I0766032

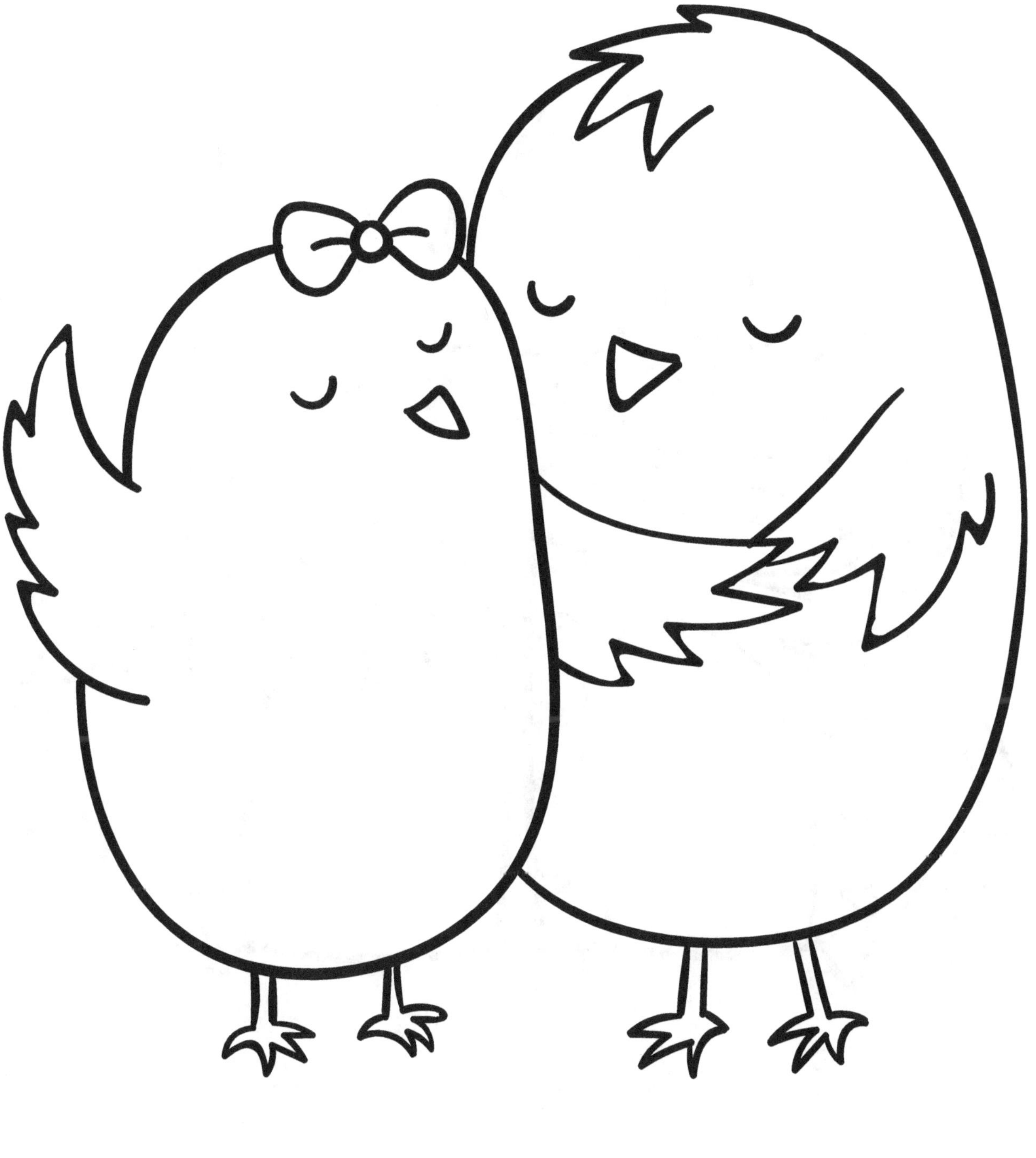

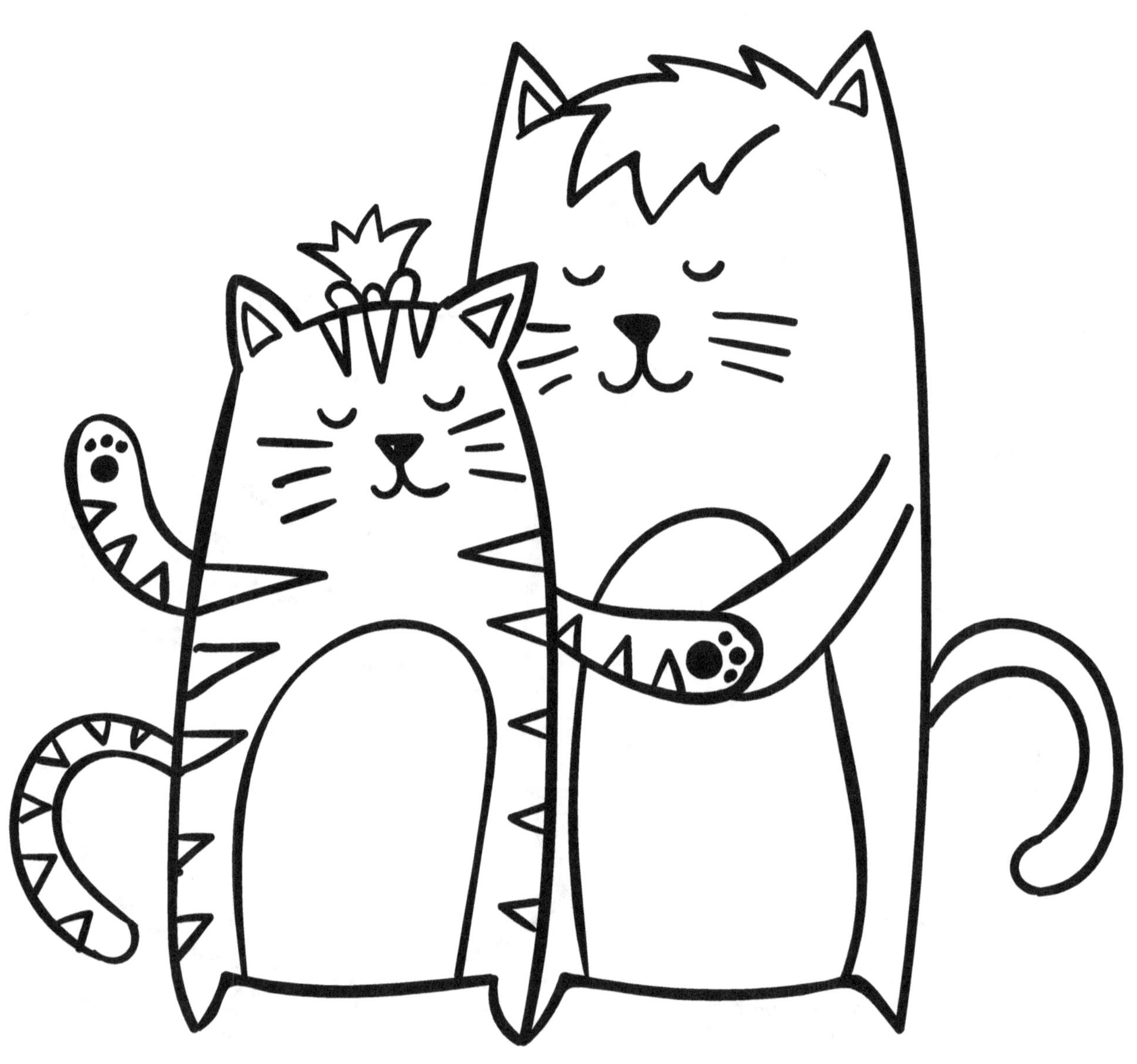

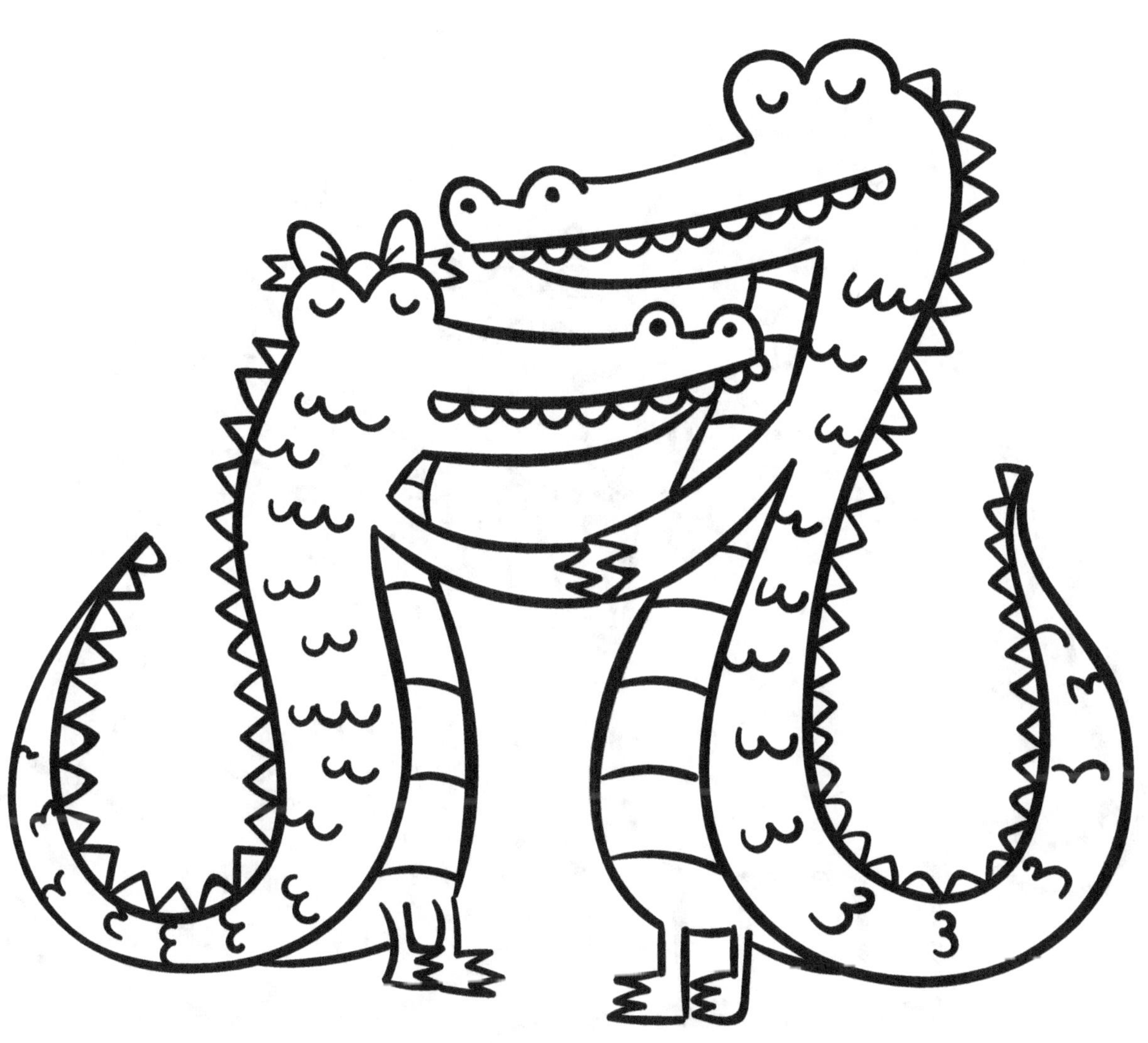

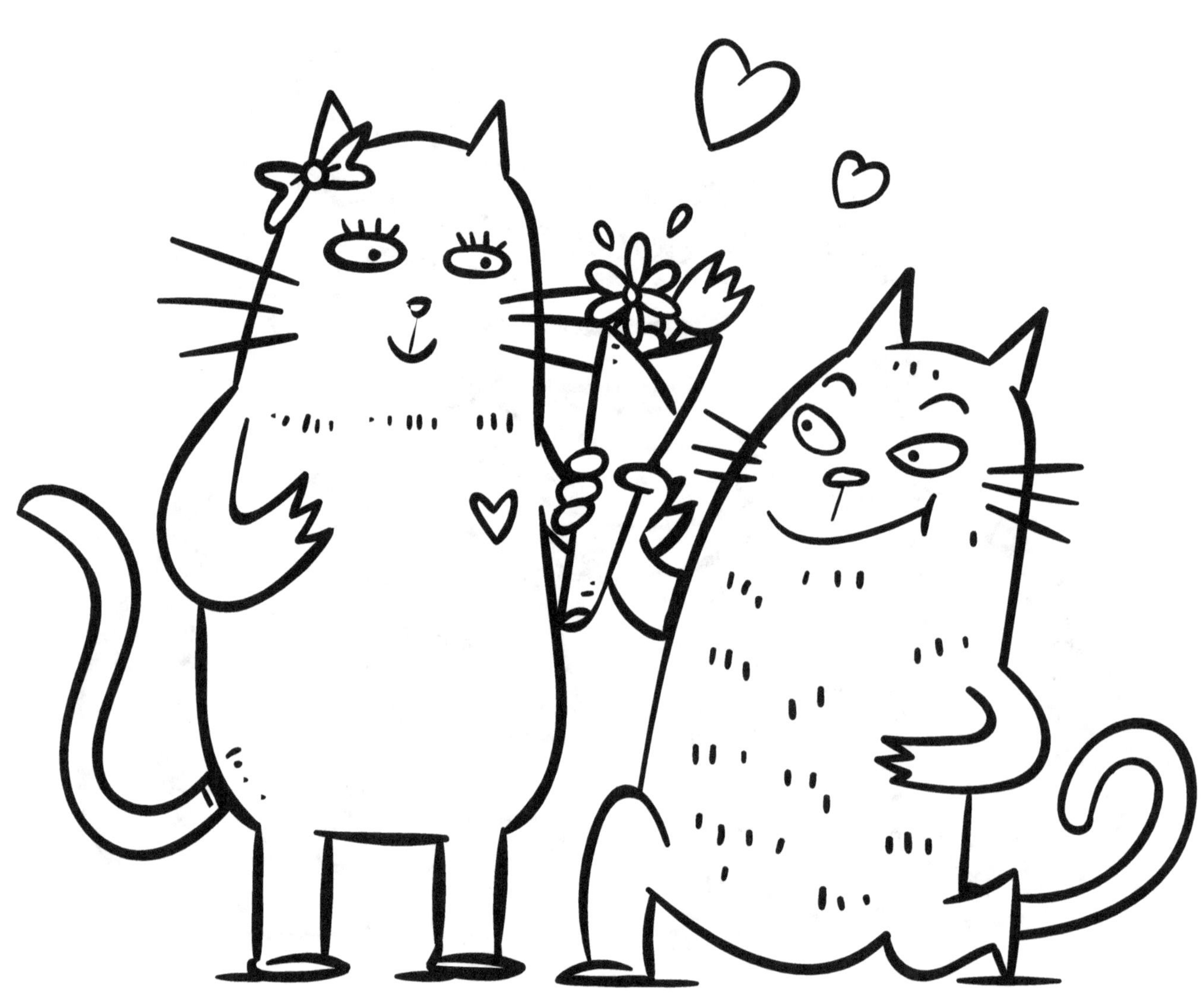

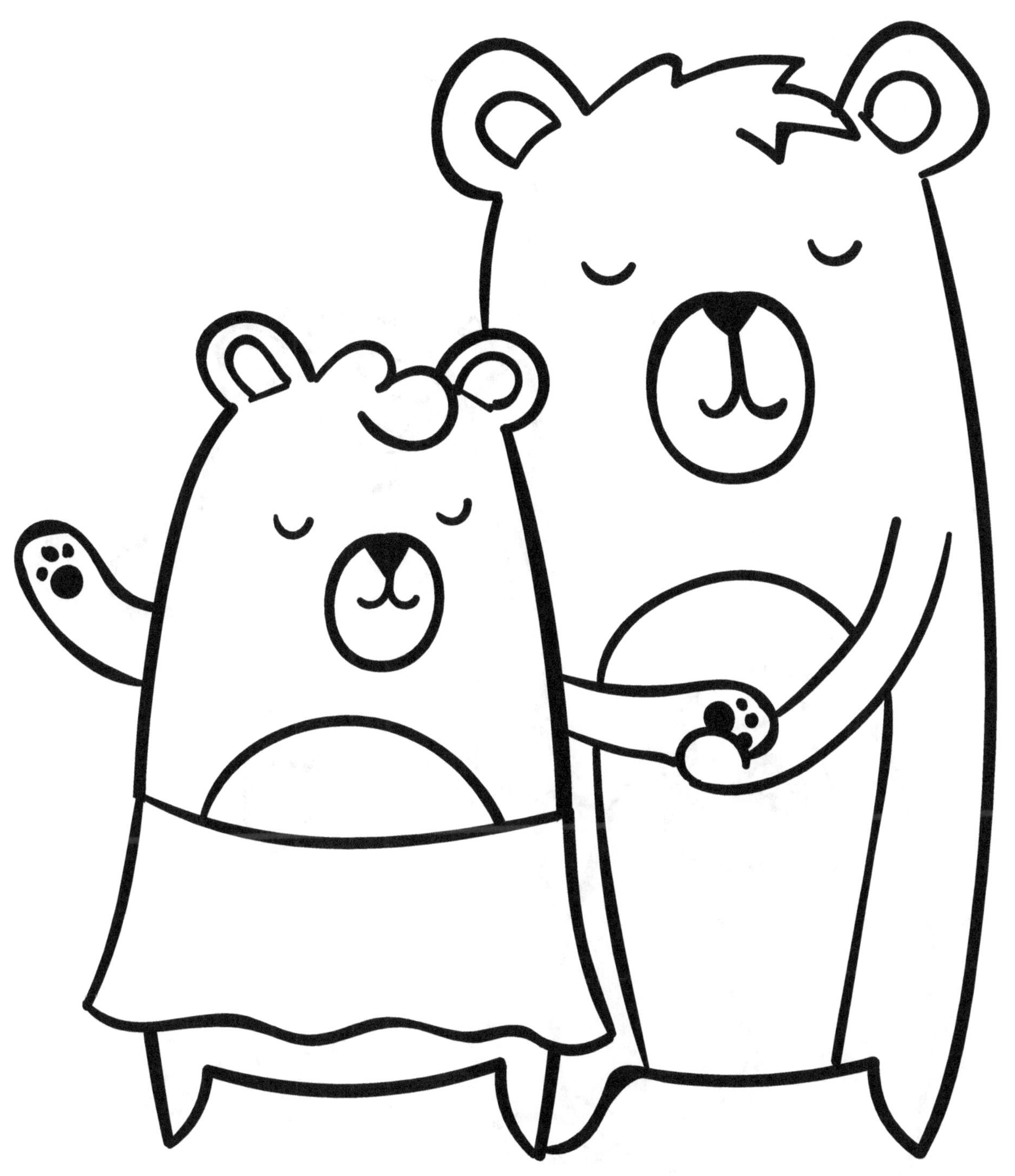

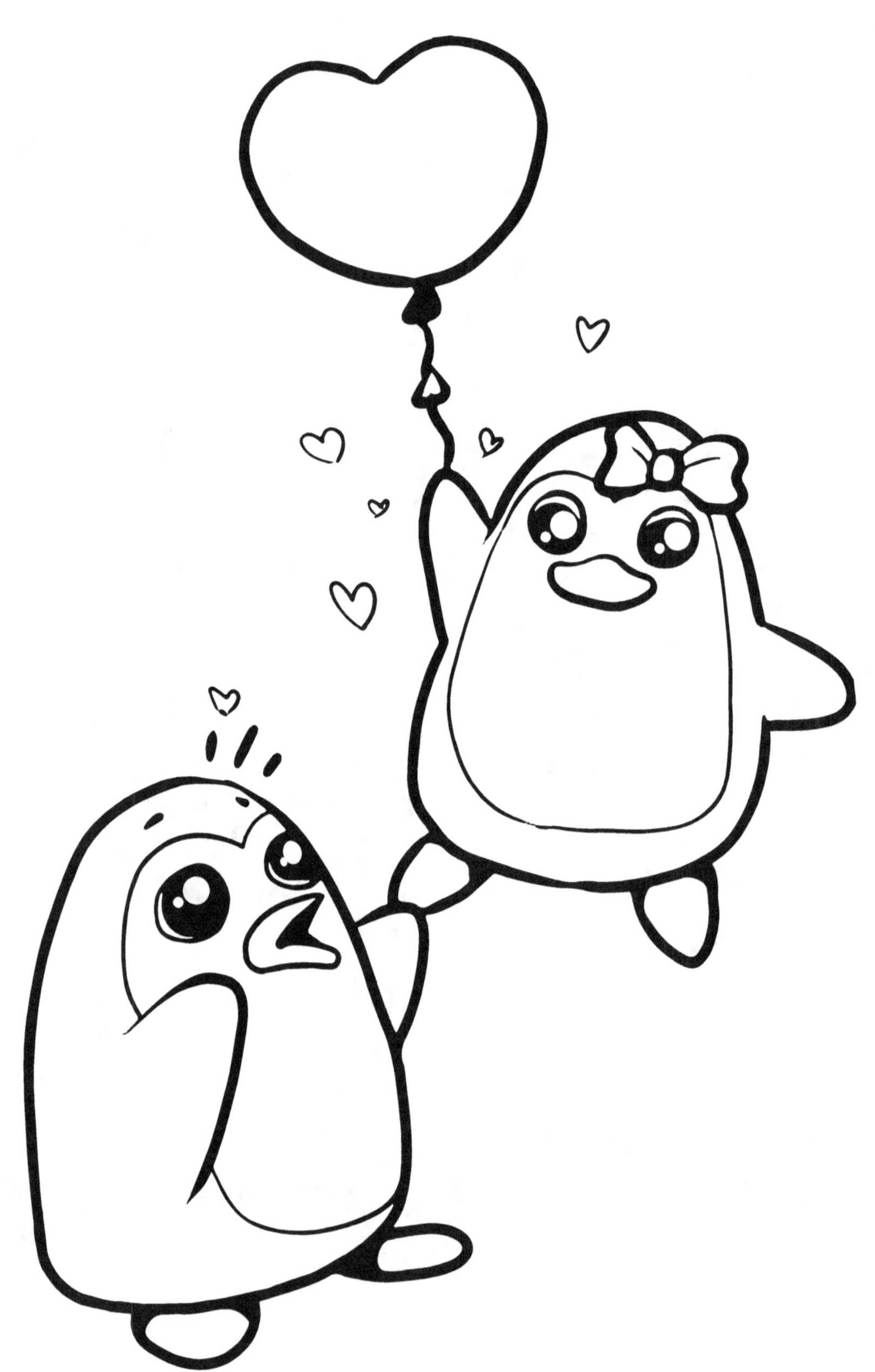

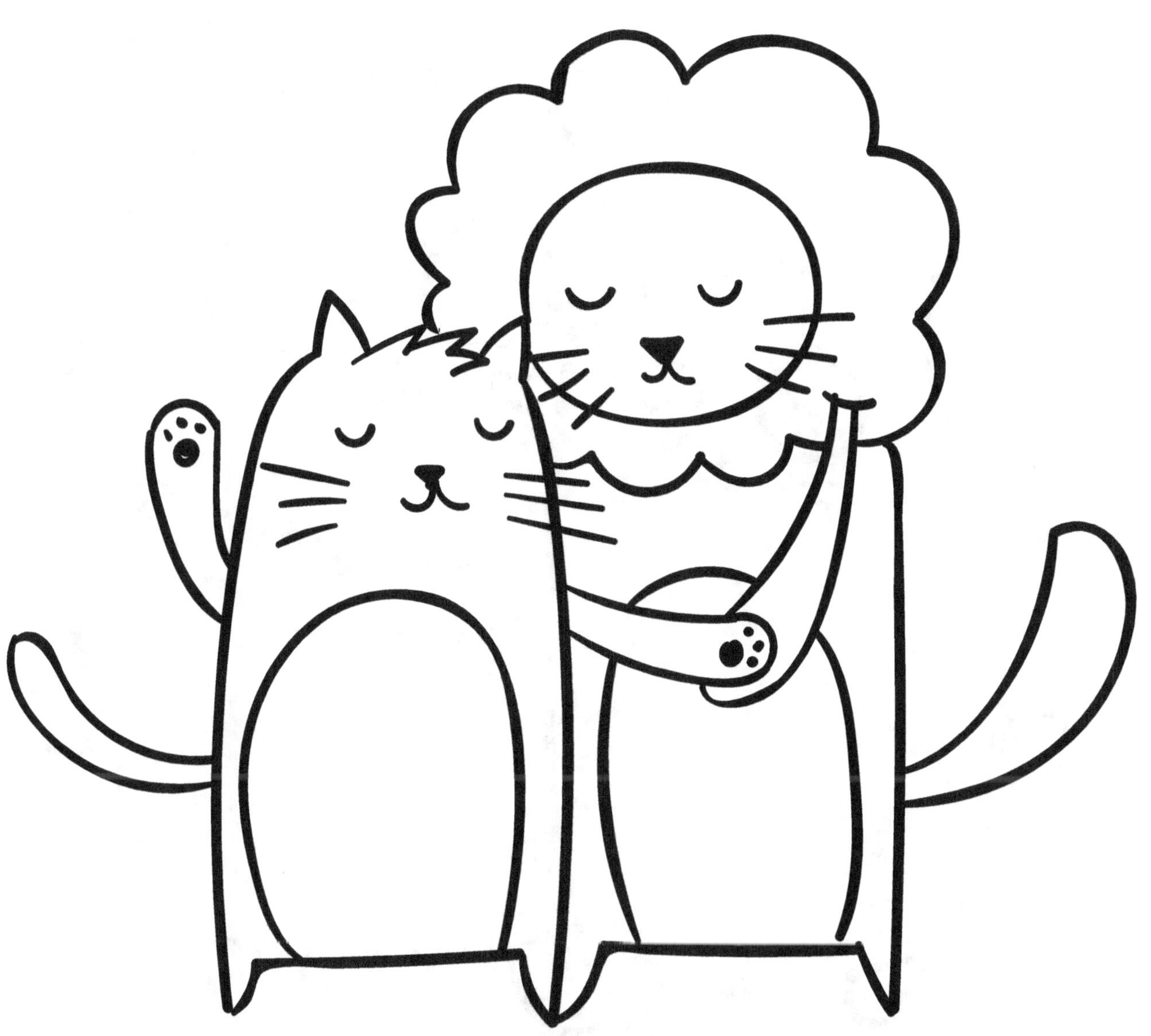

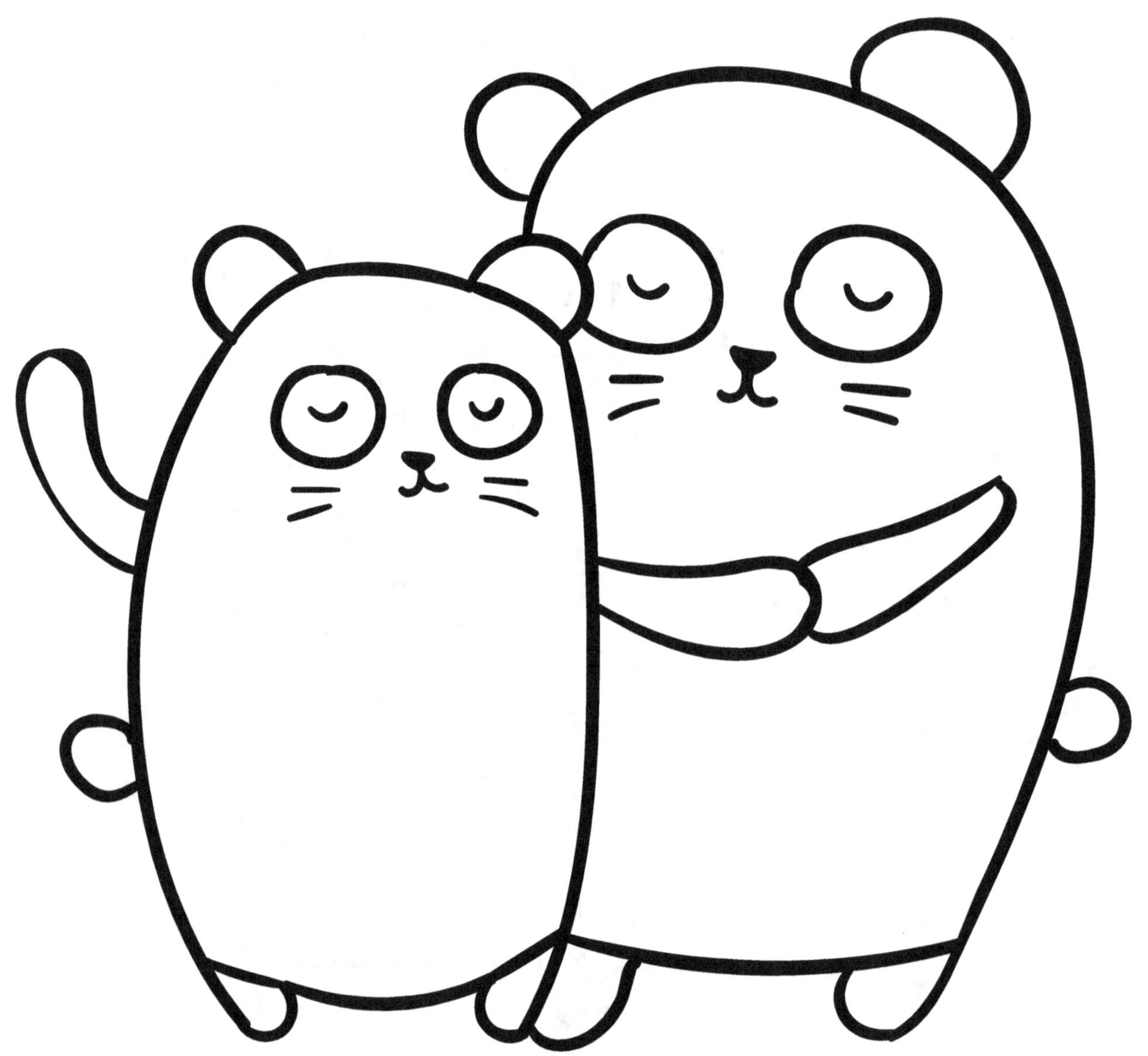

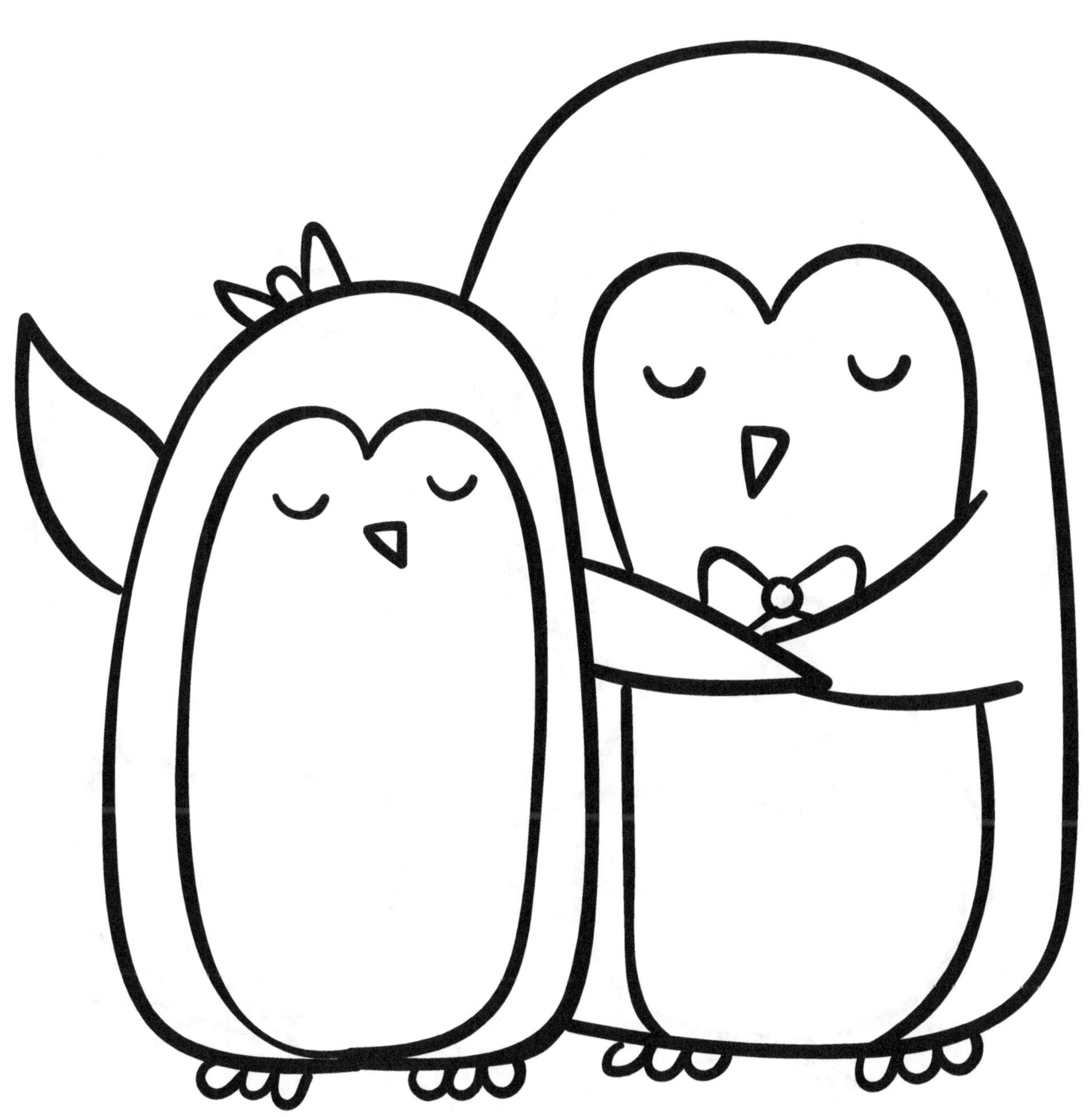

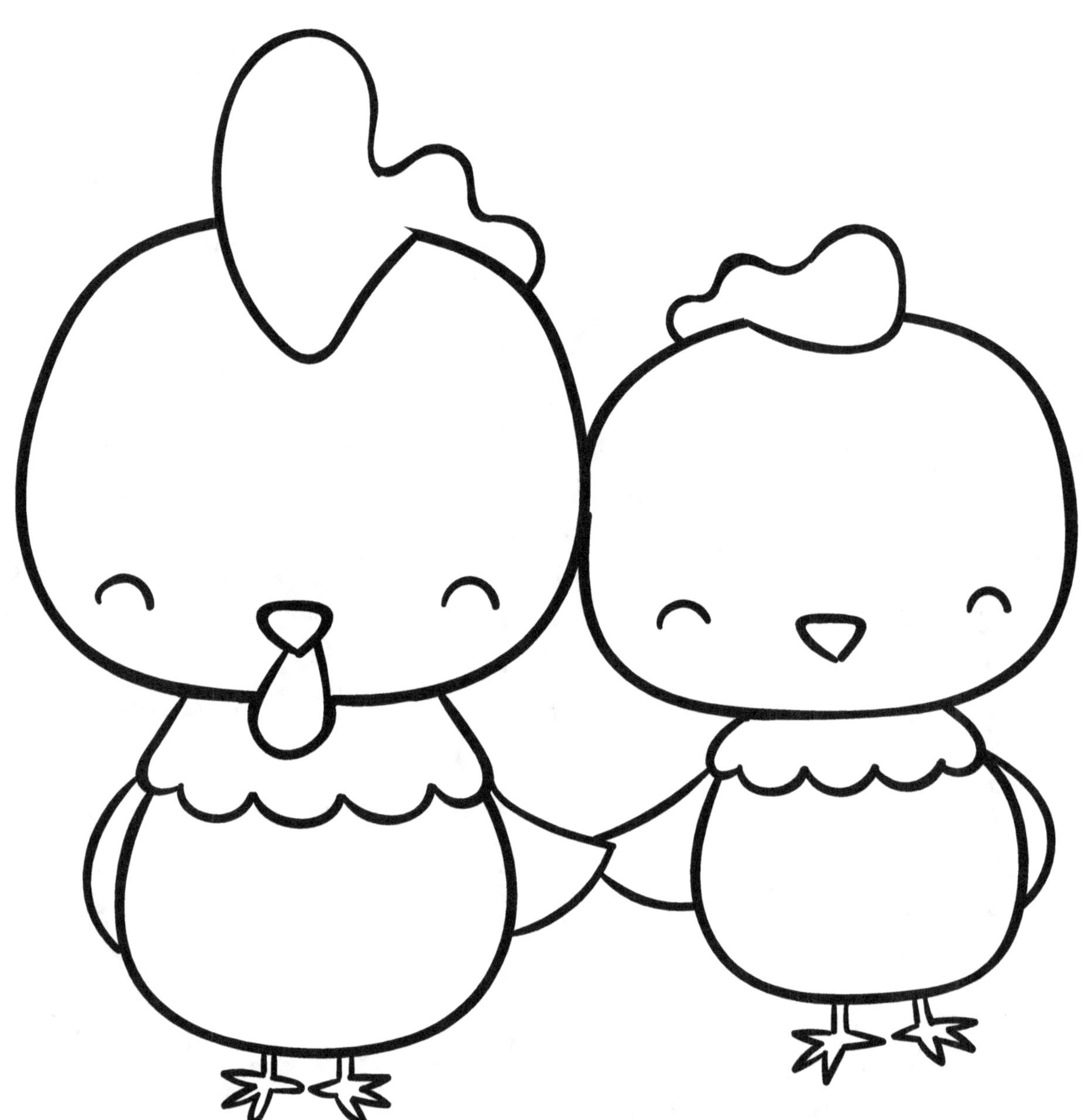

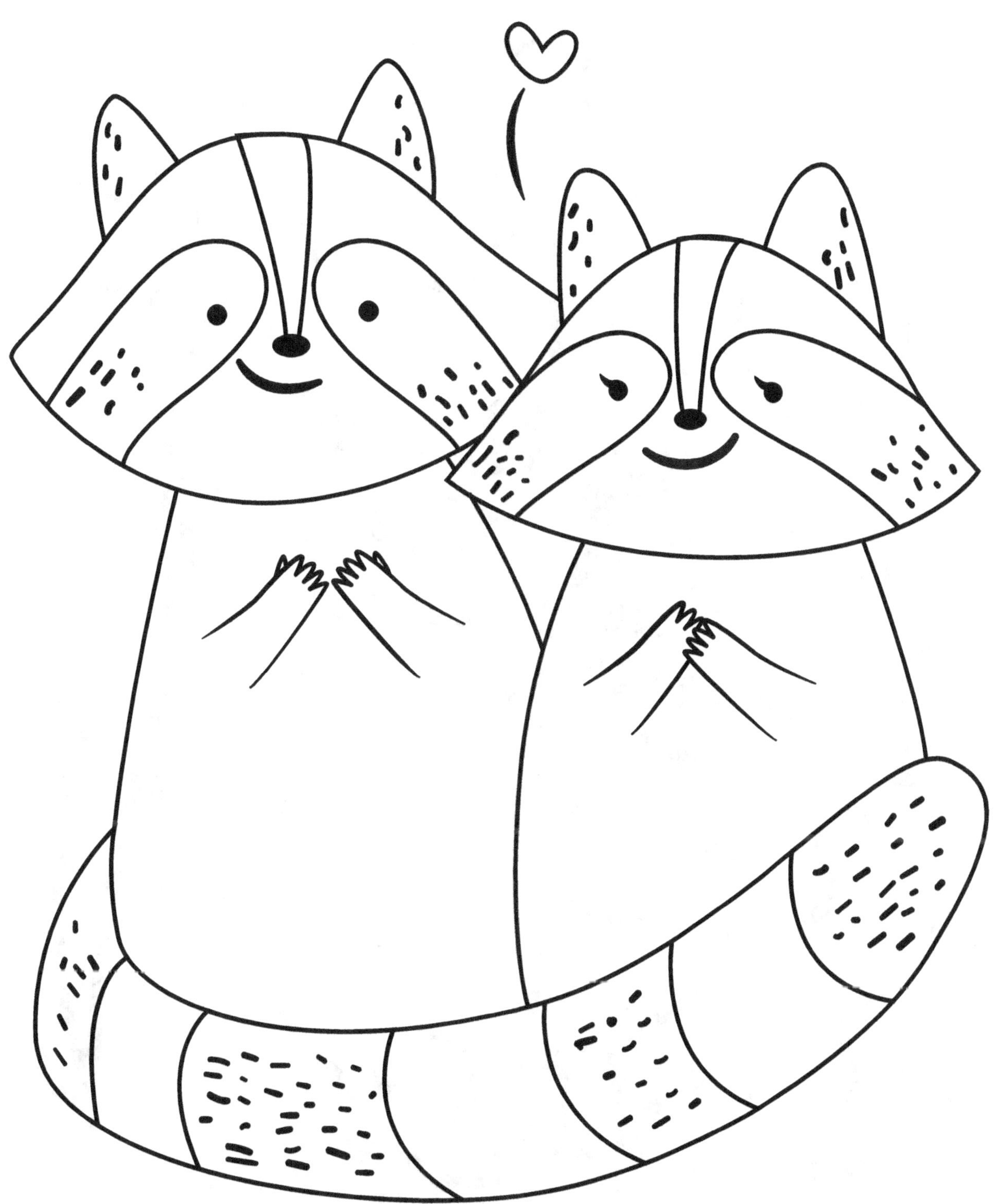

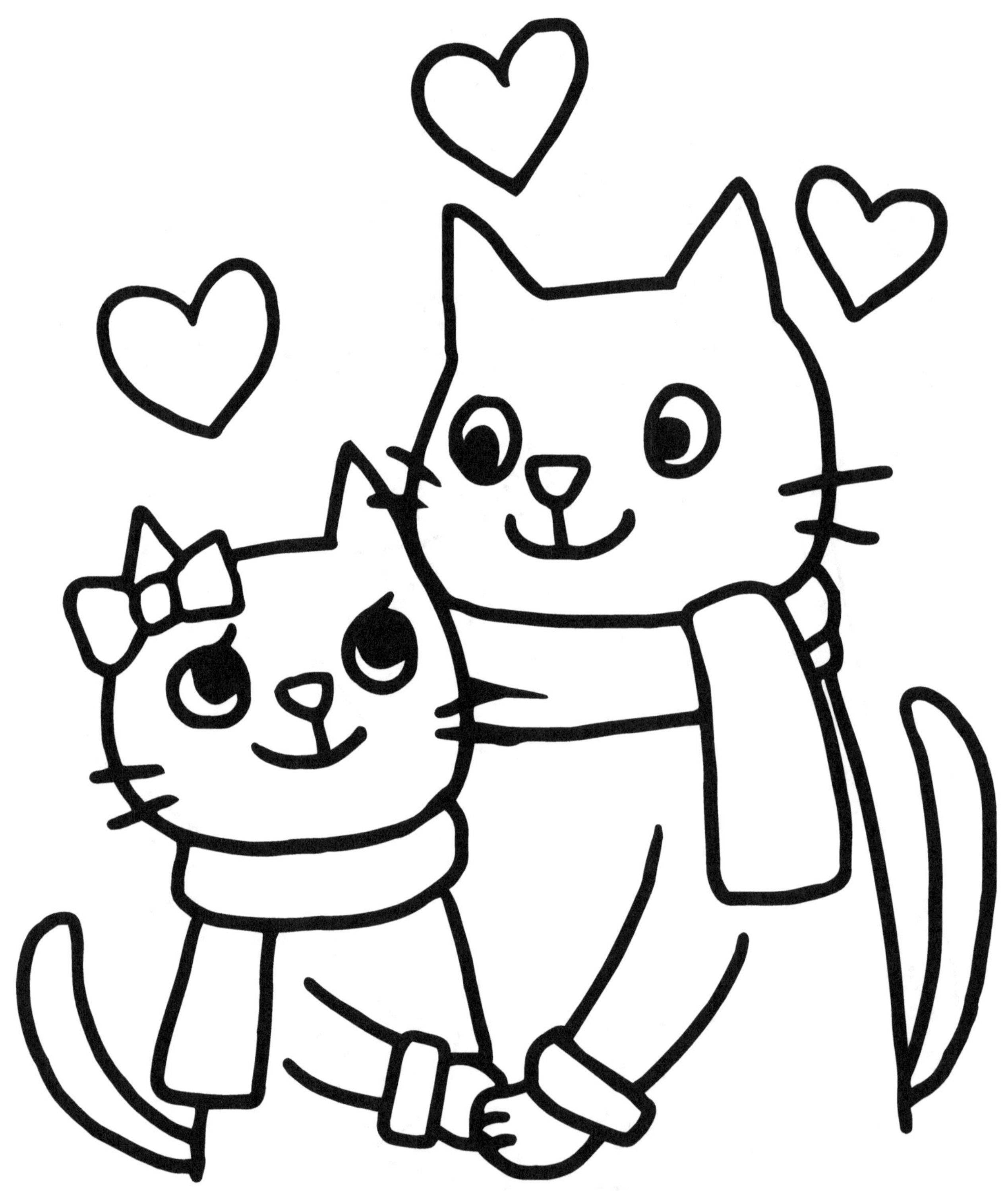

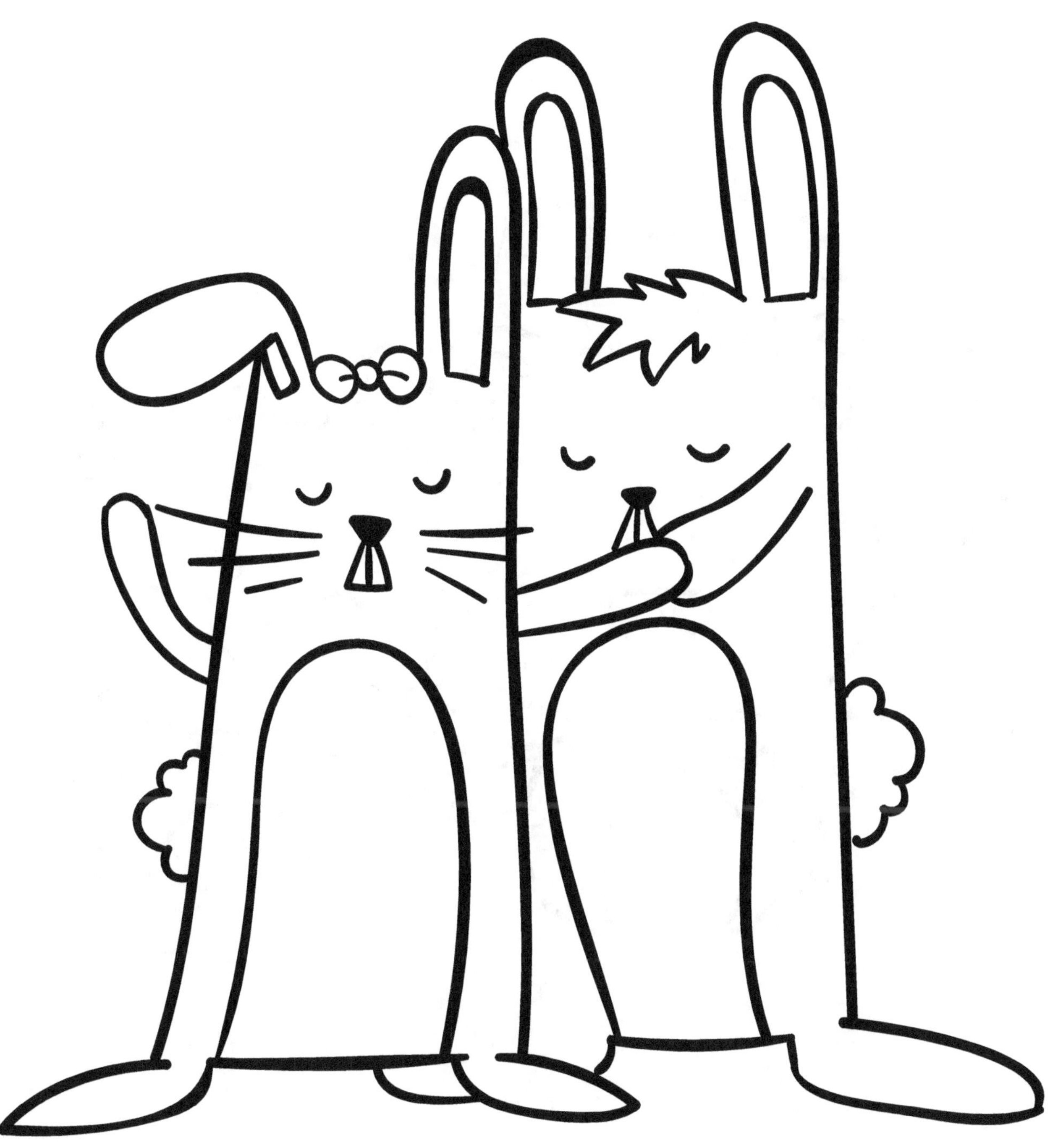

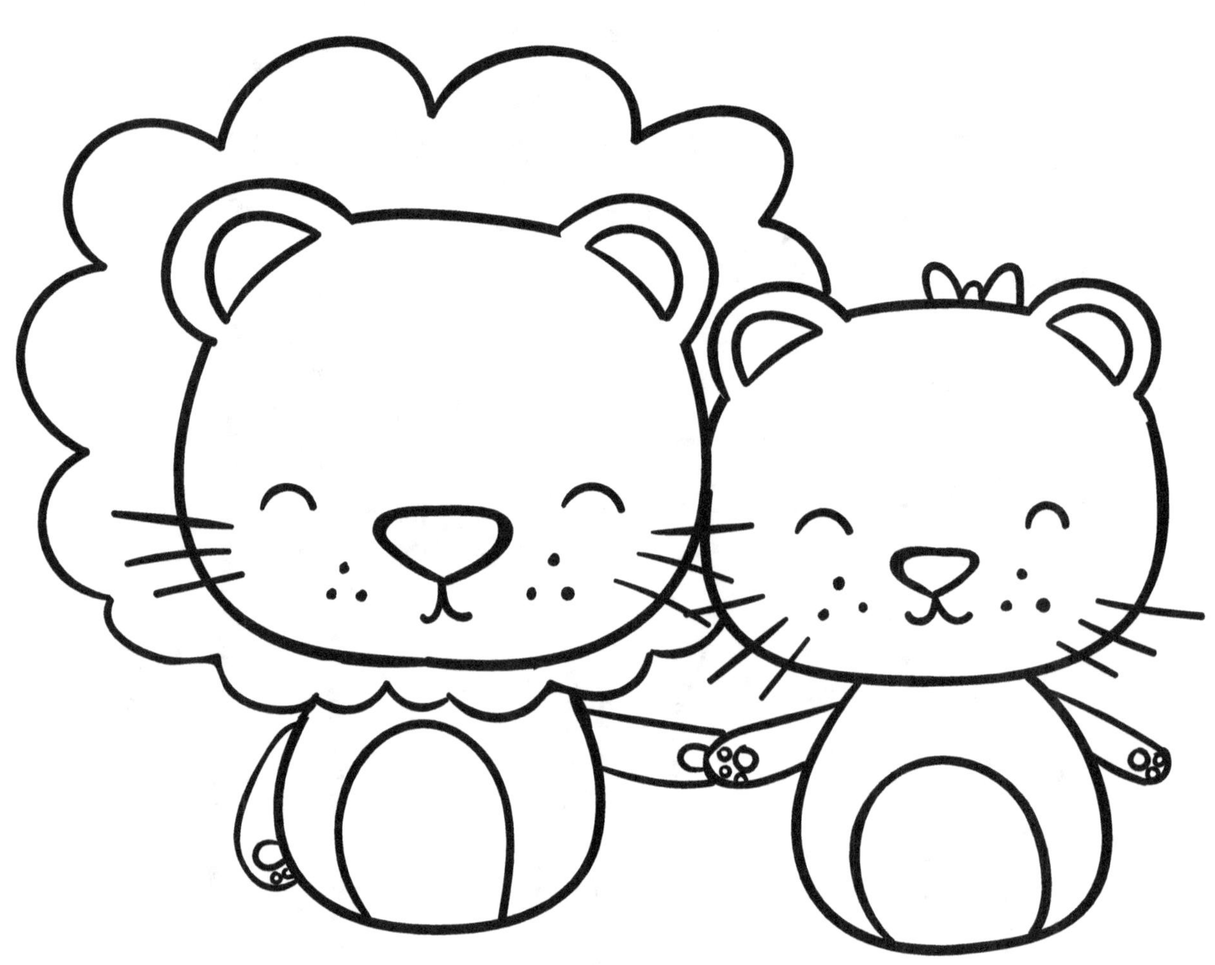

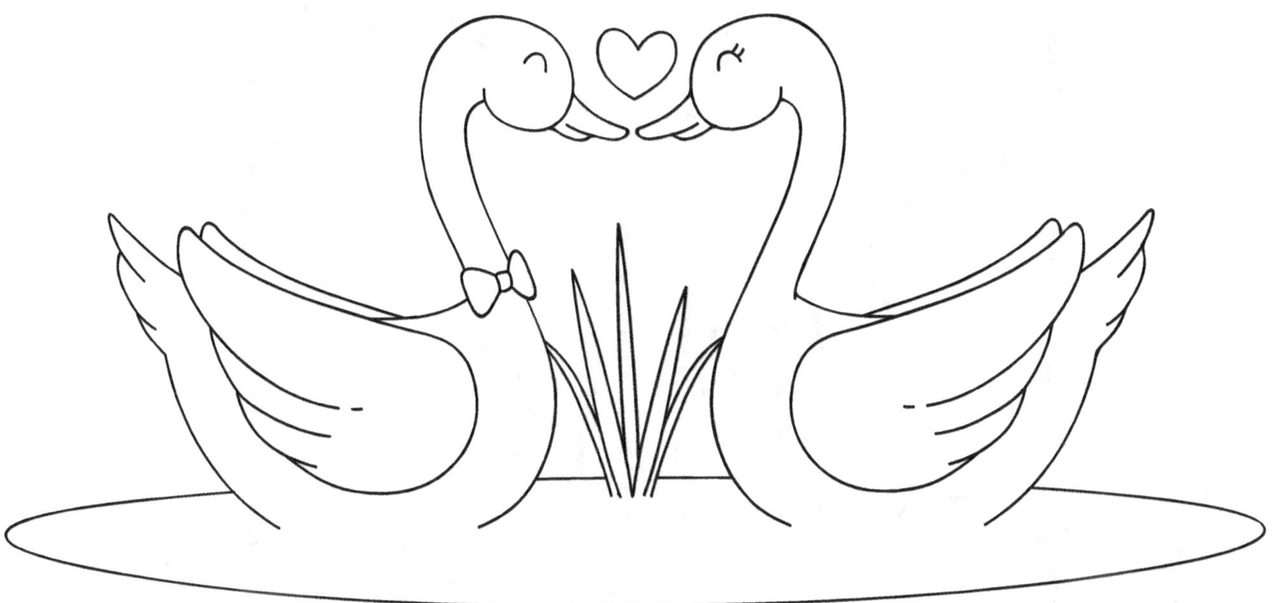

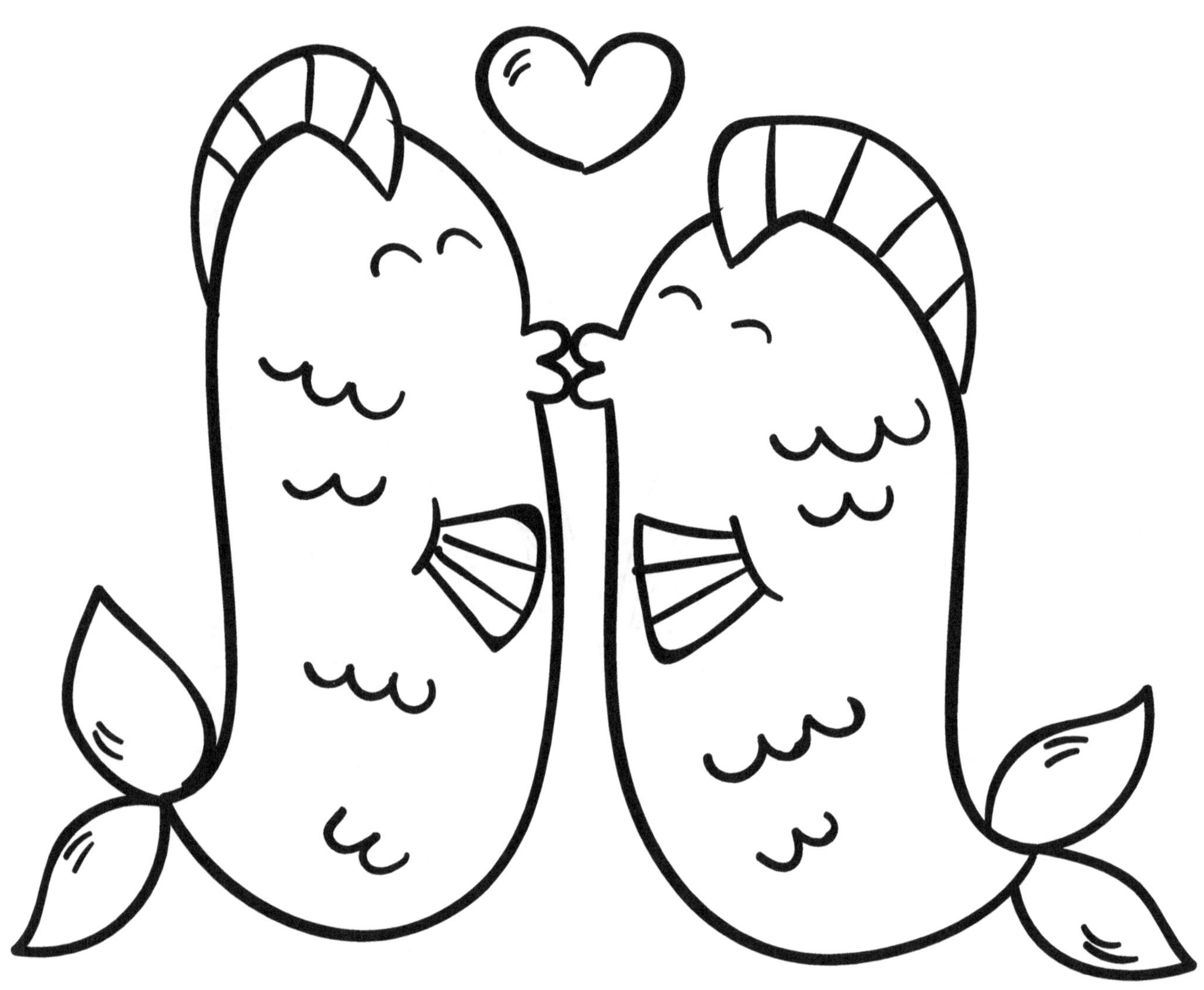

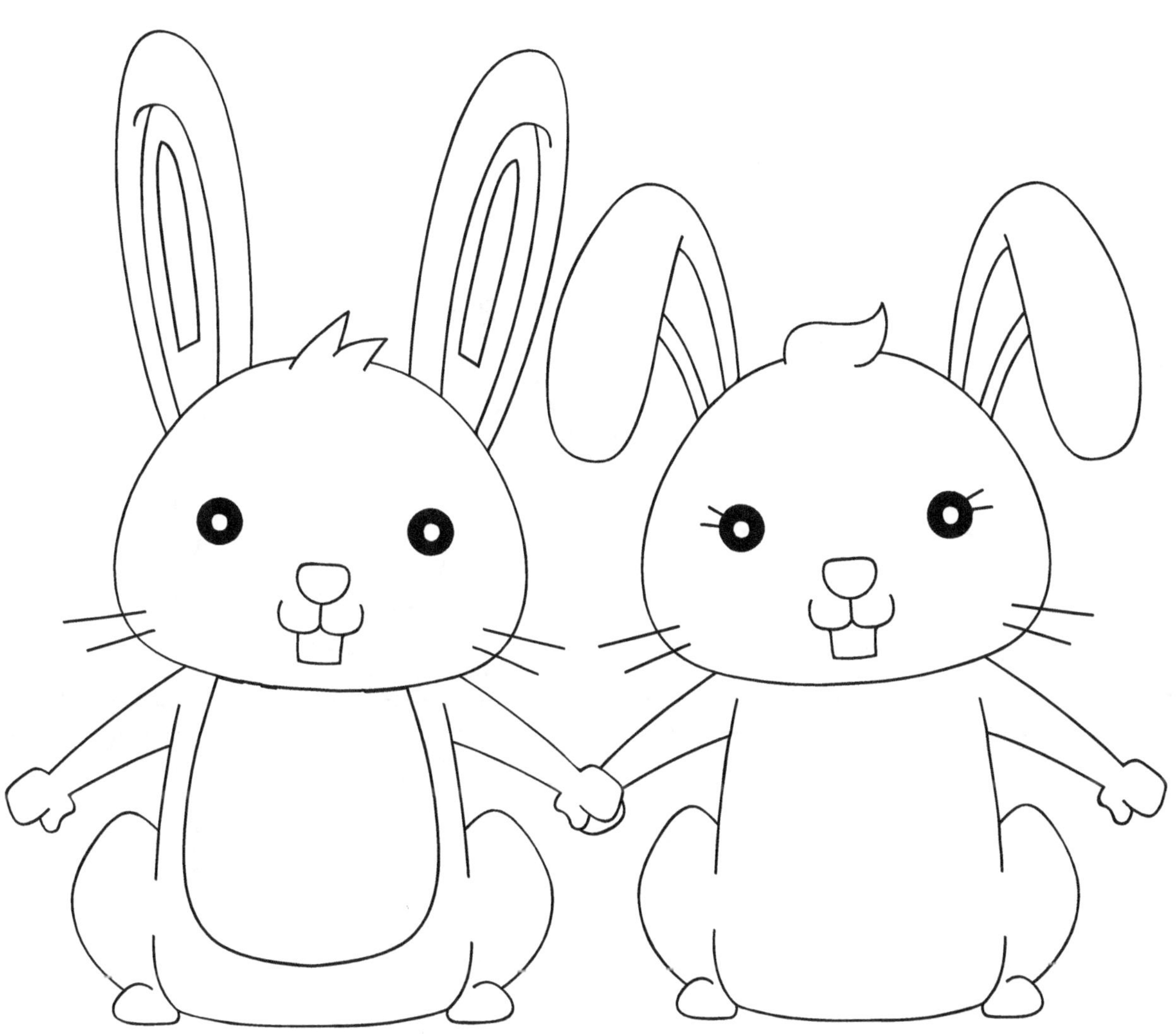

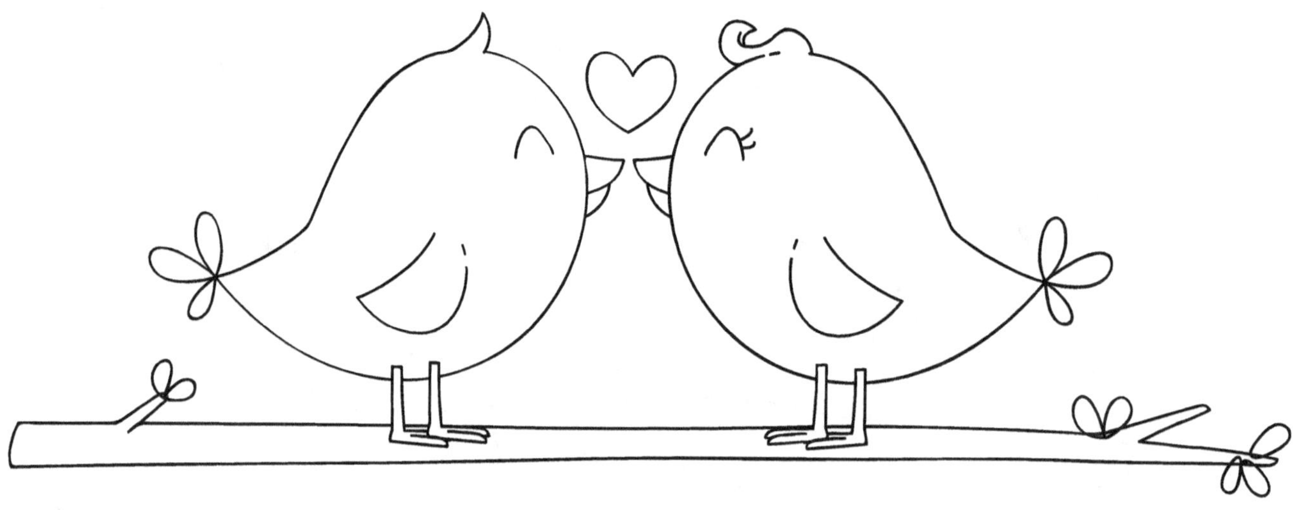

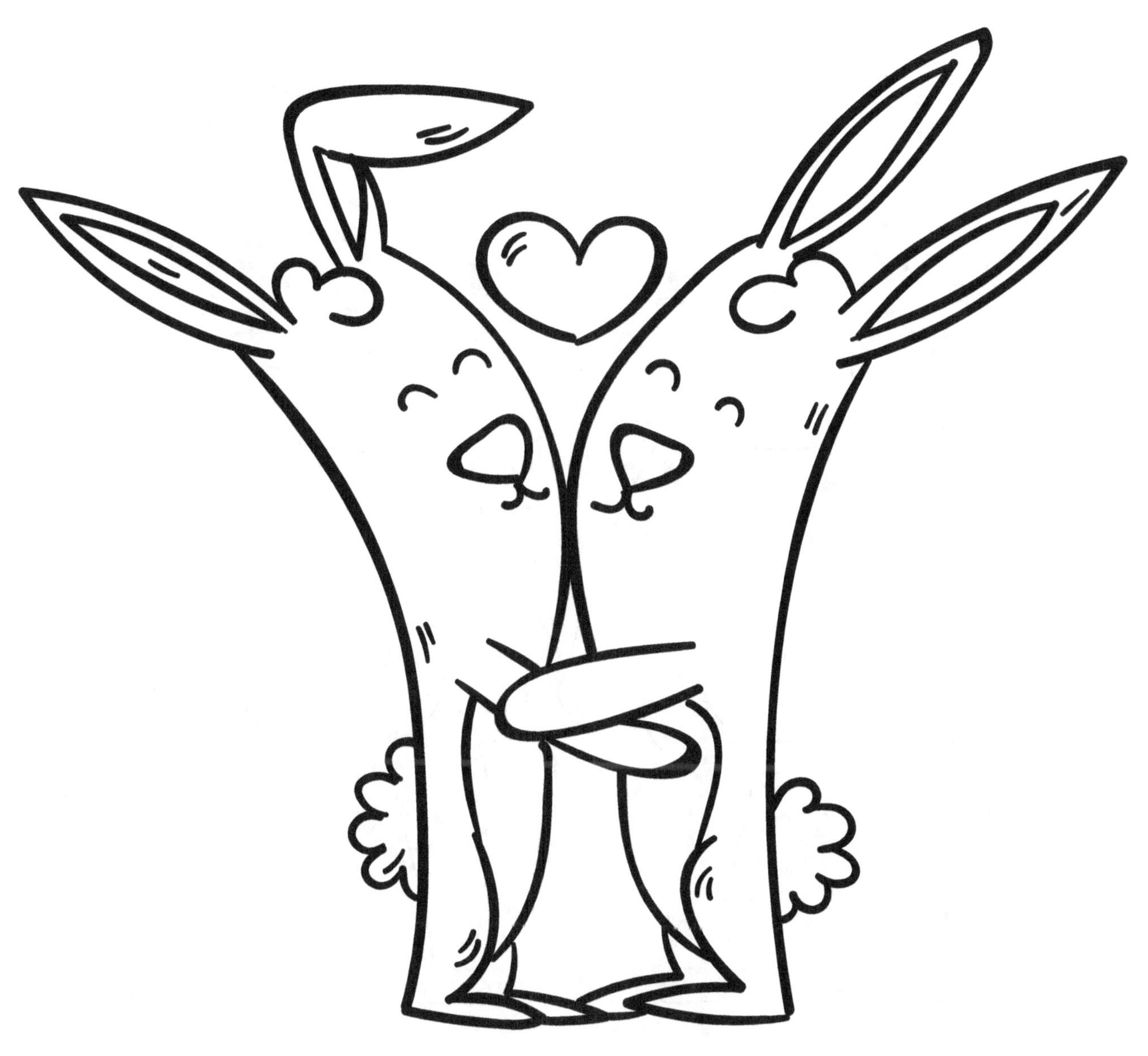

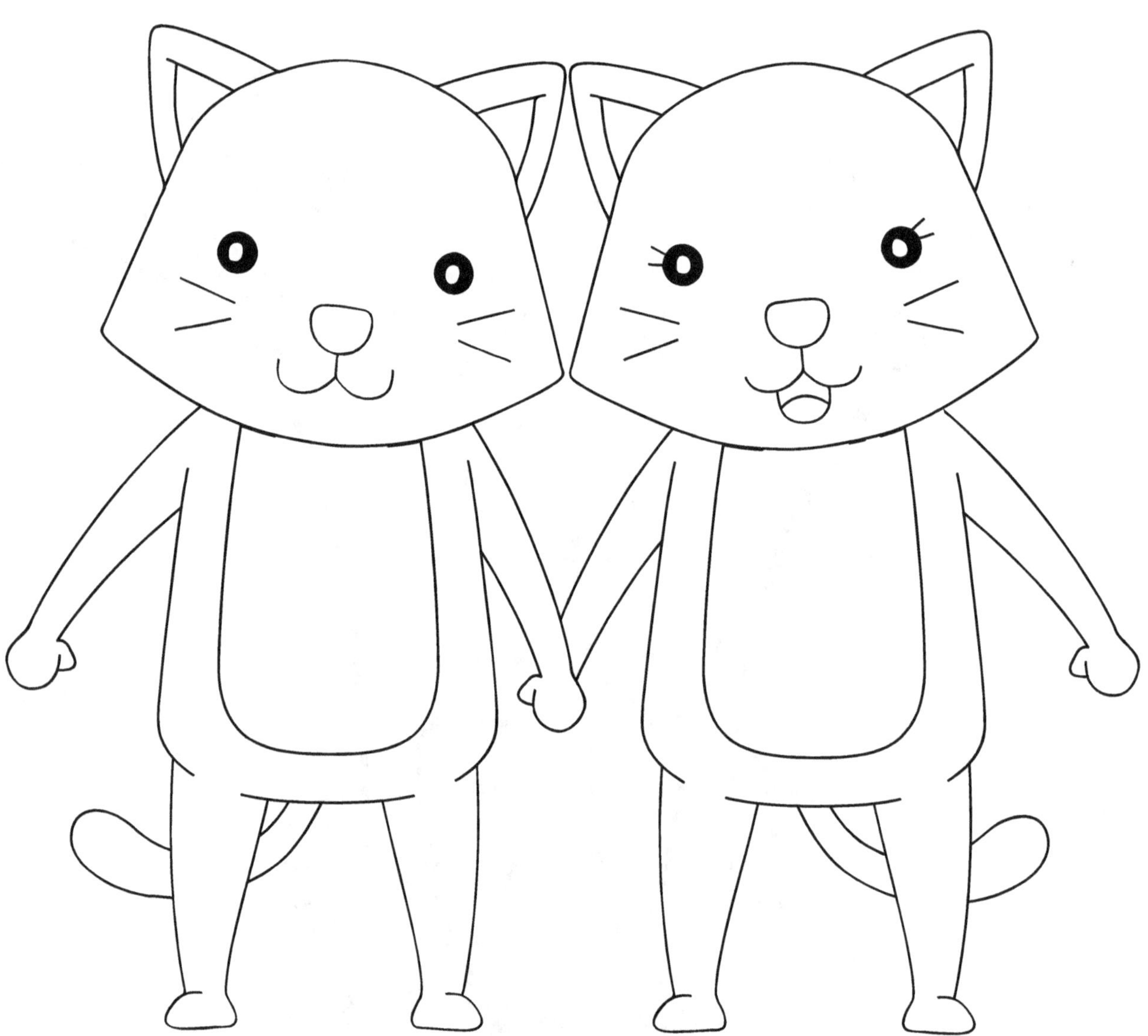

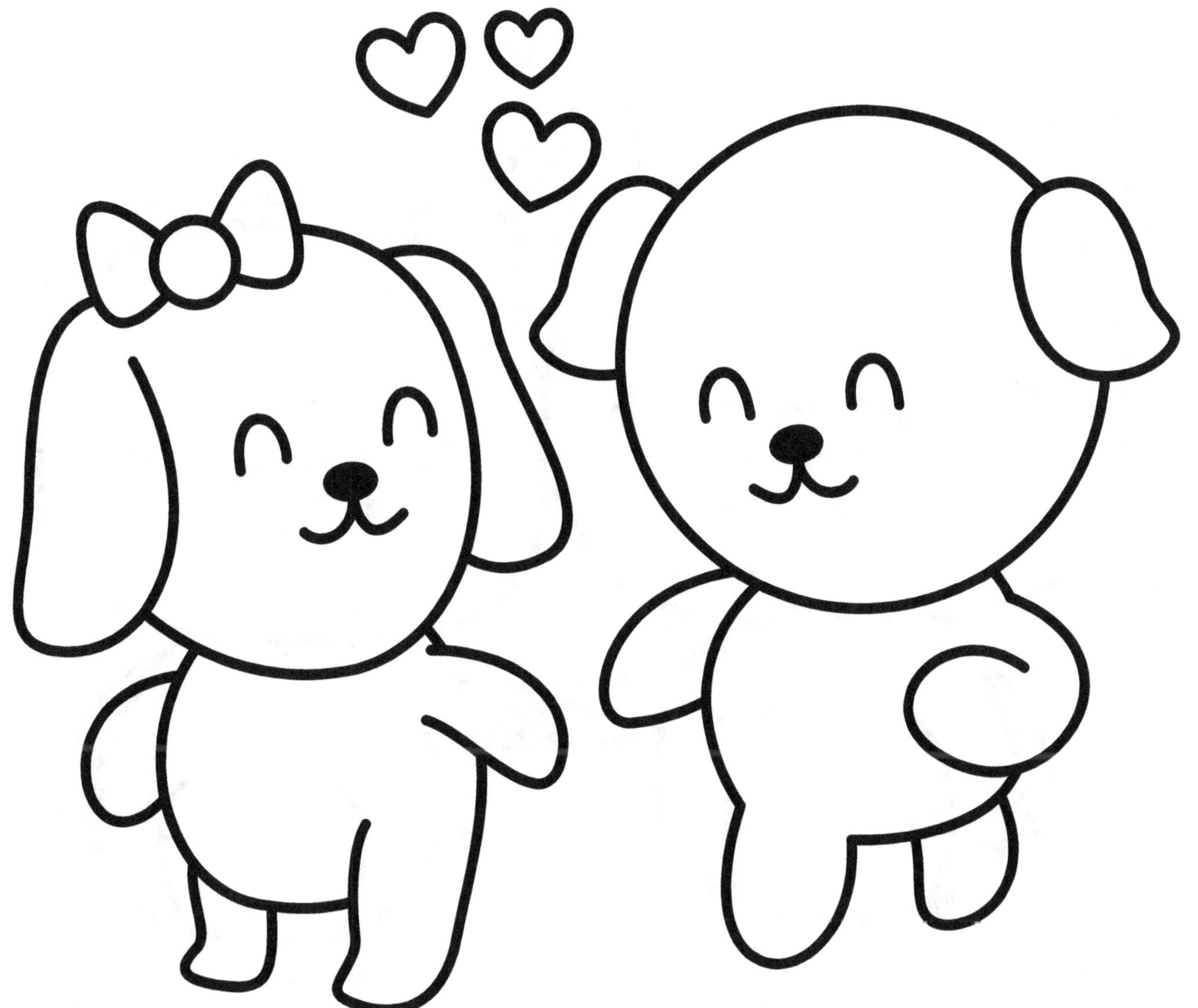

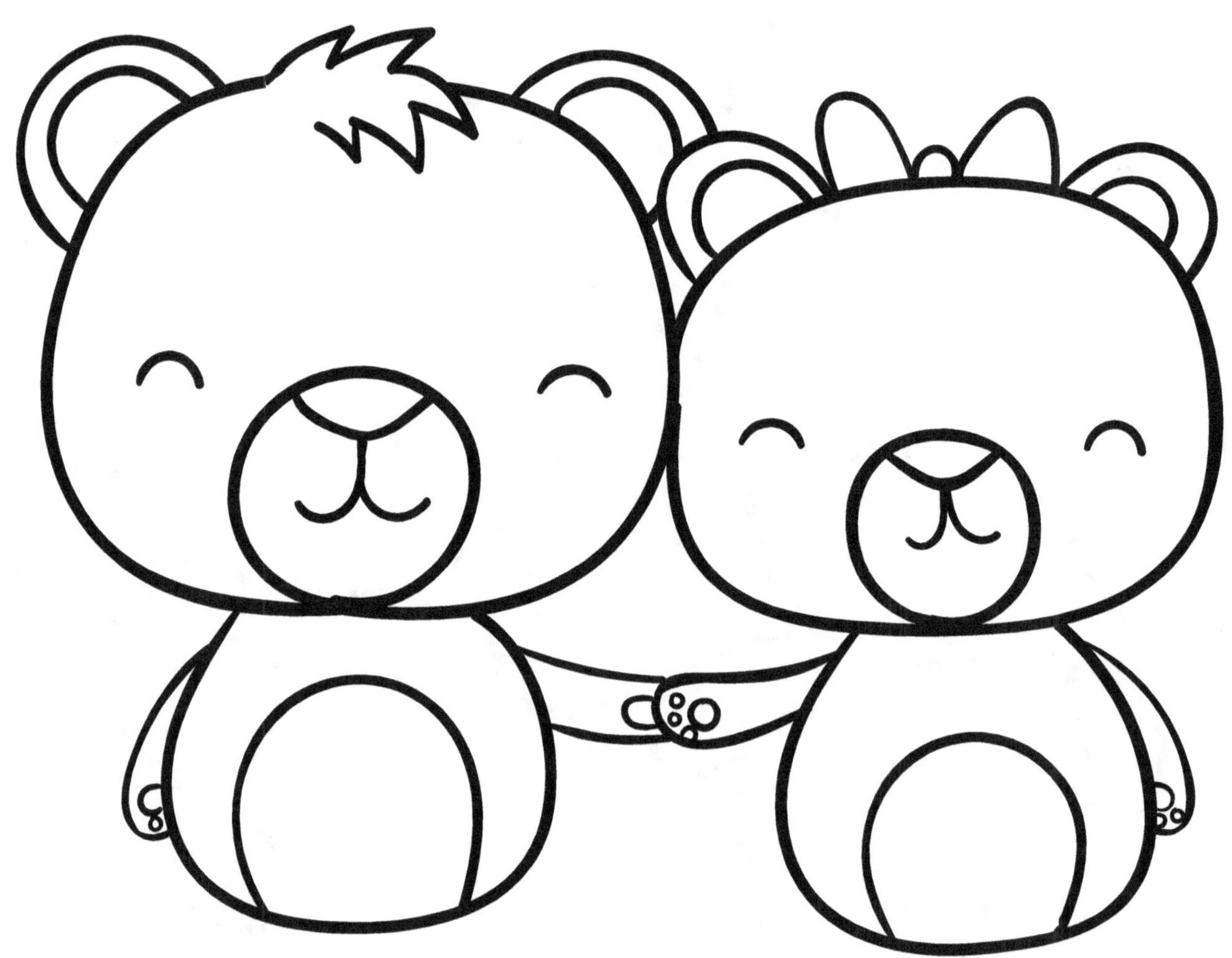

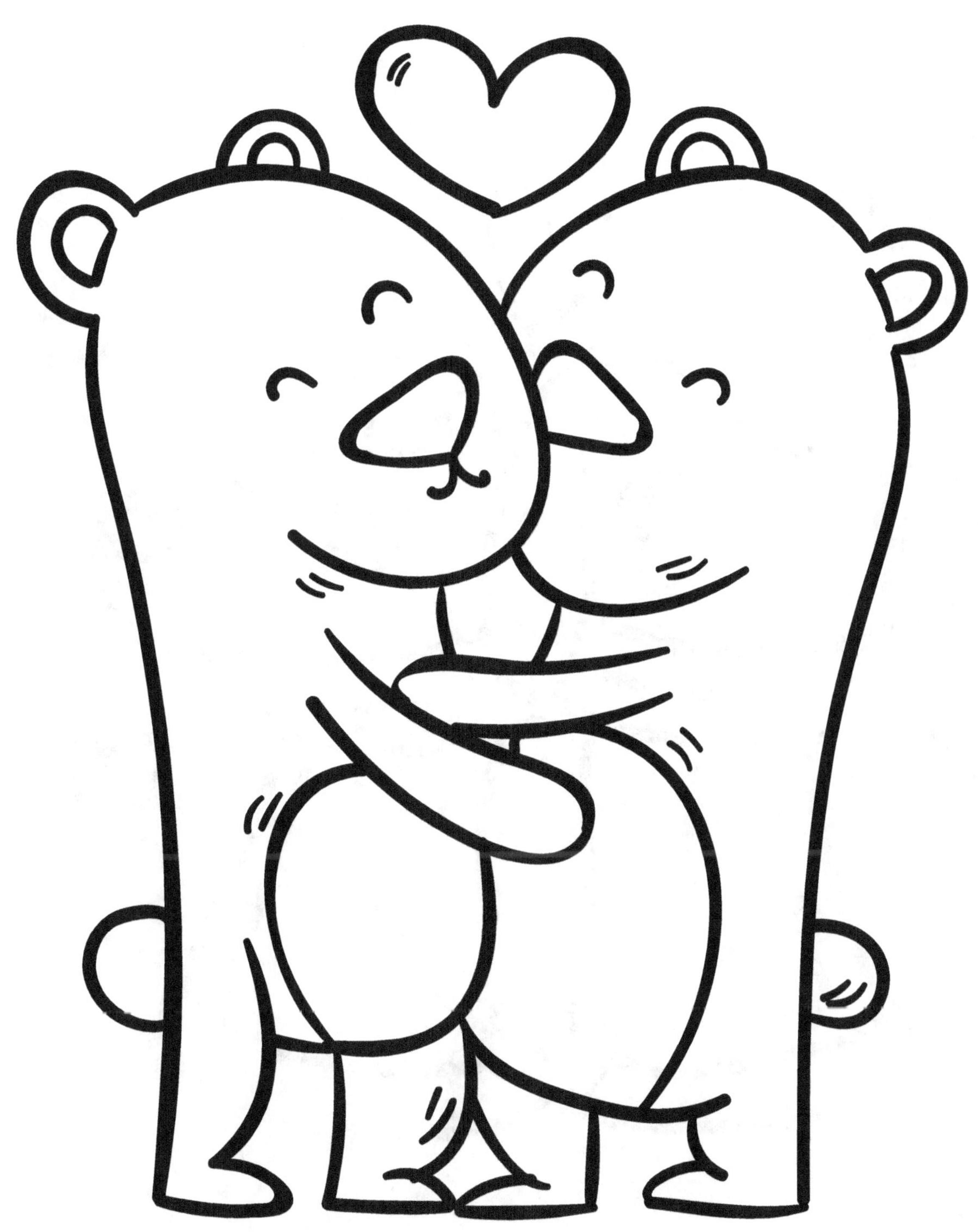

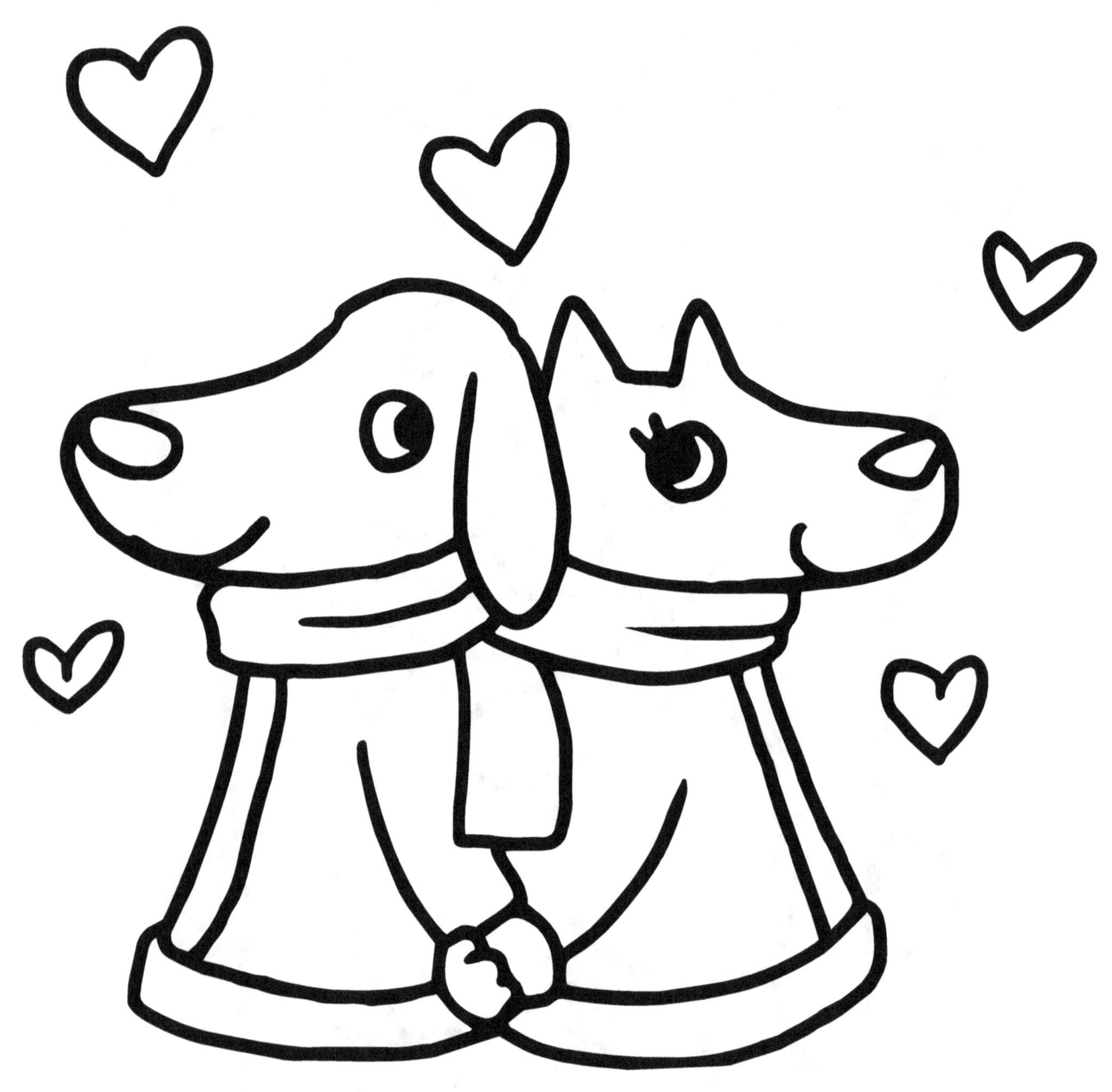

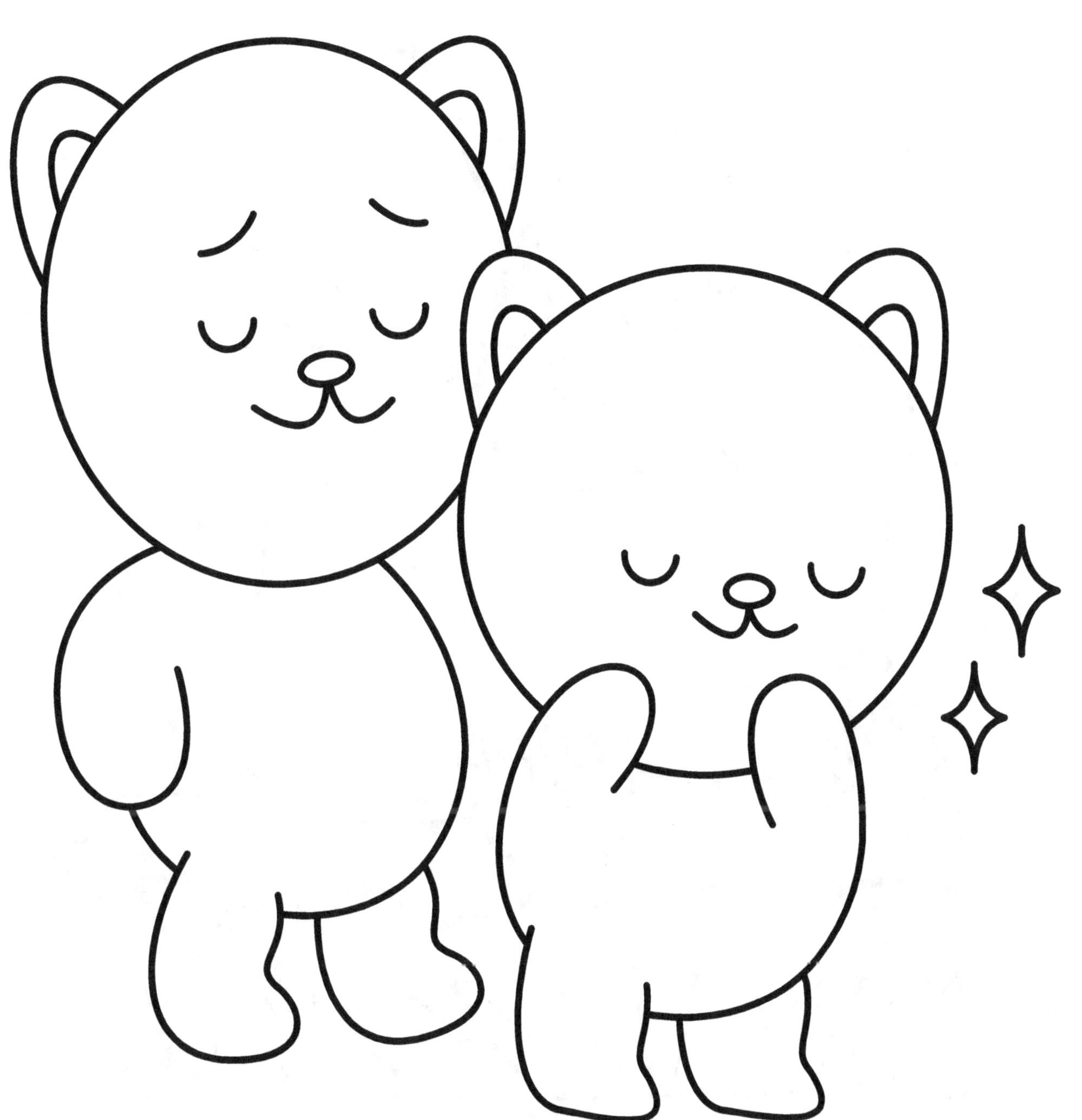

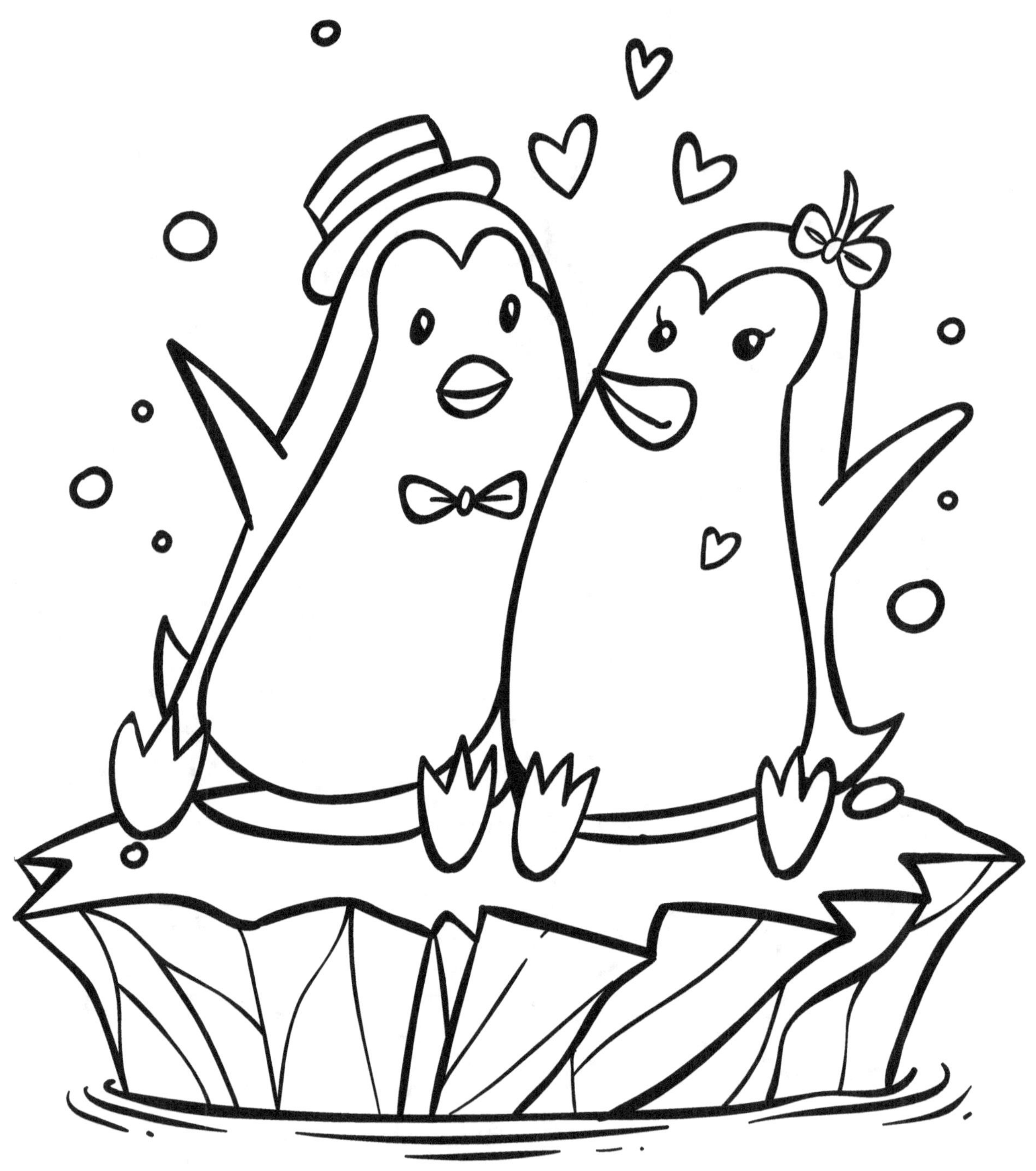

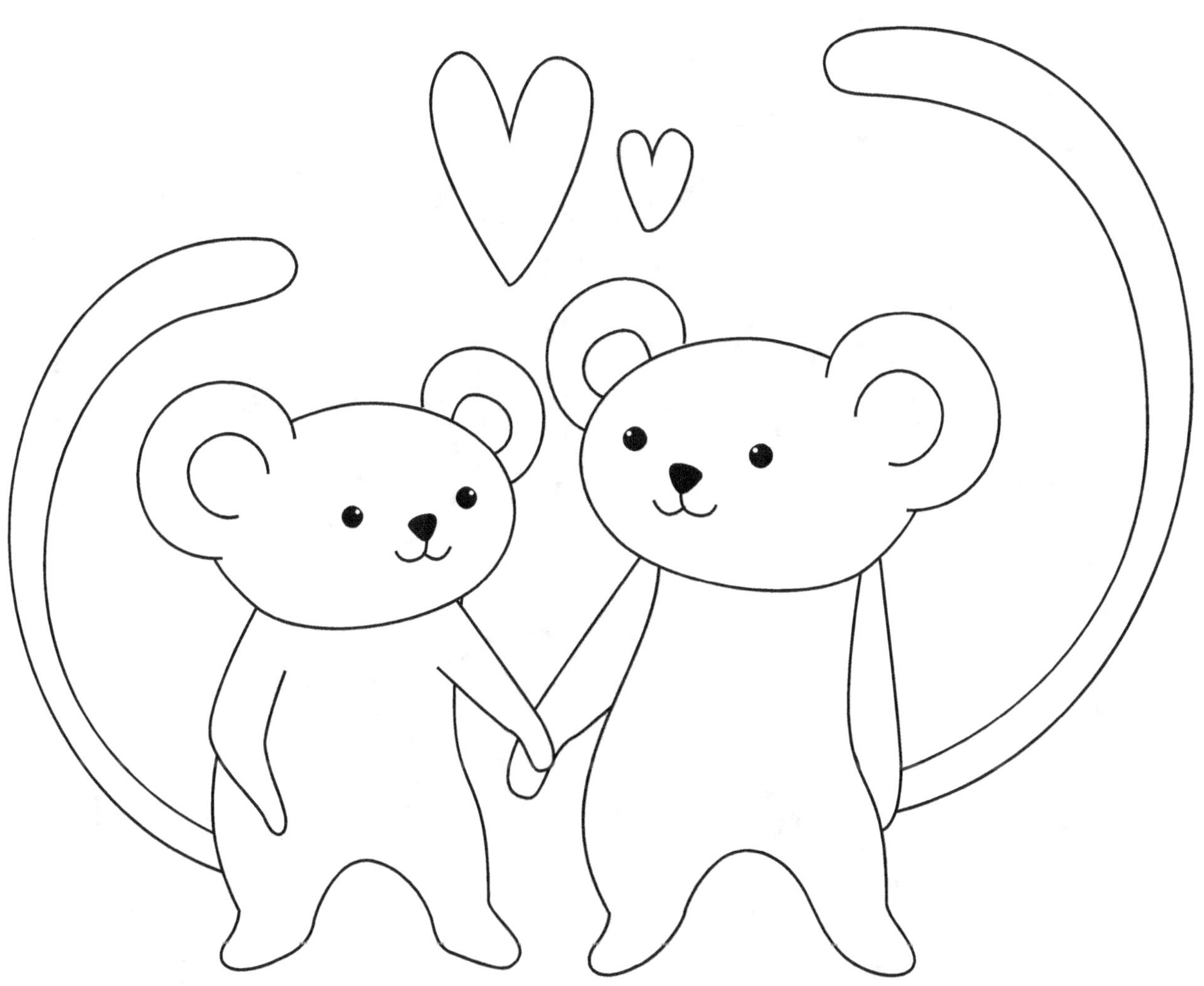

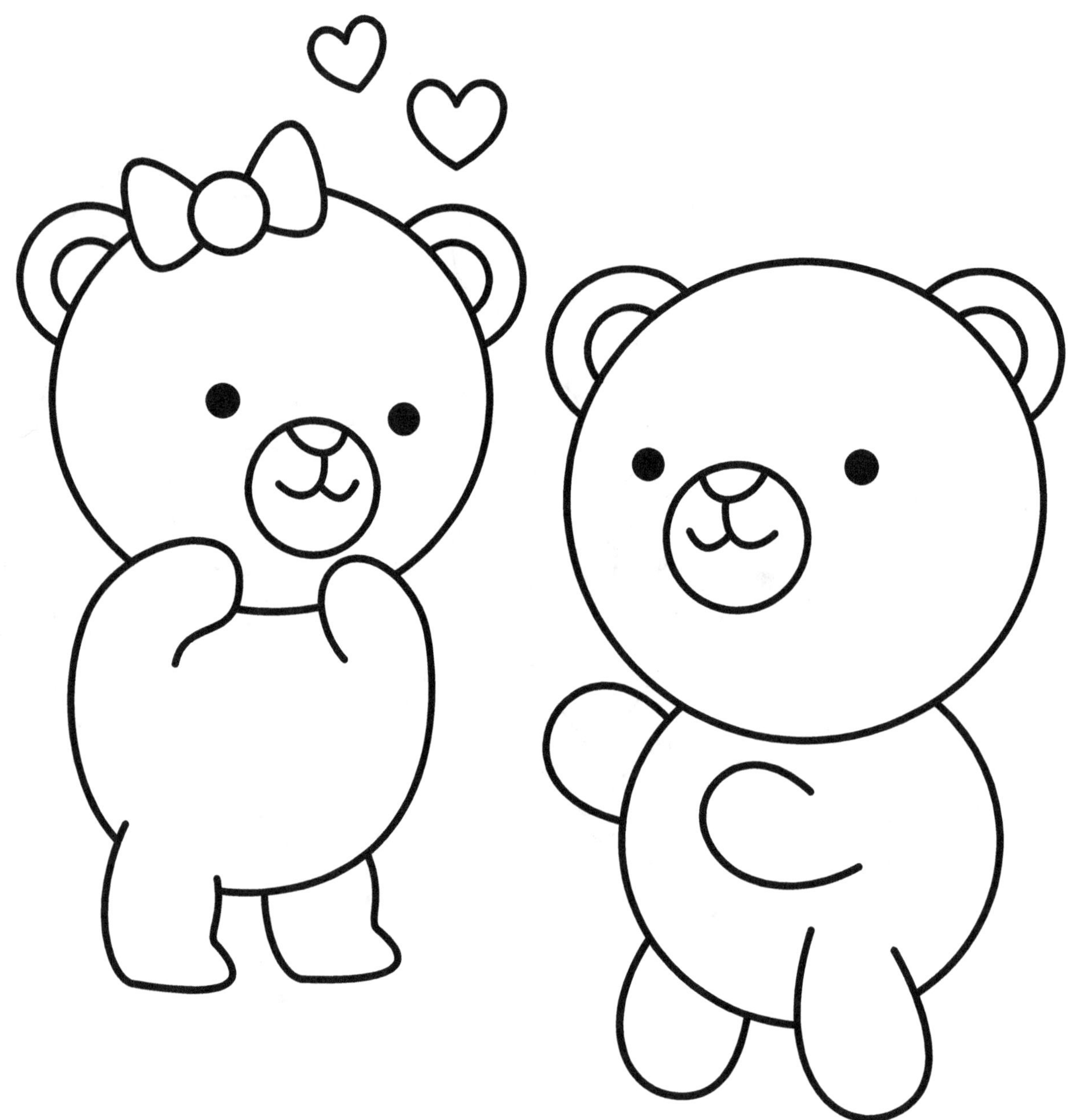

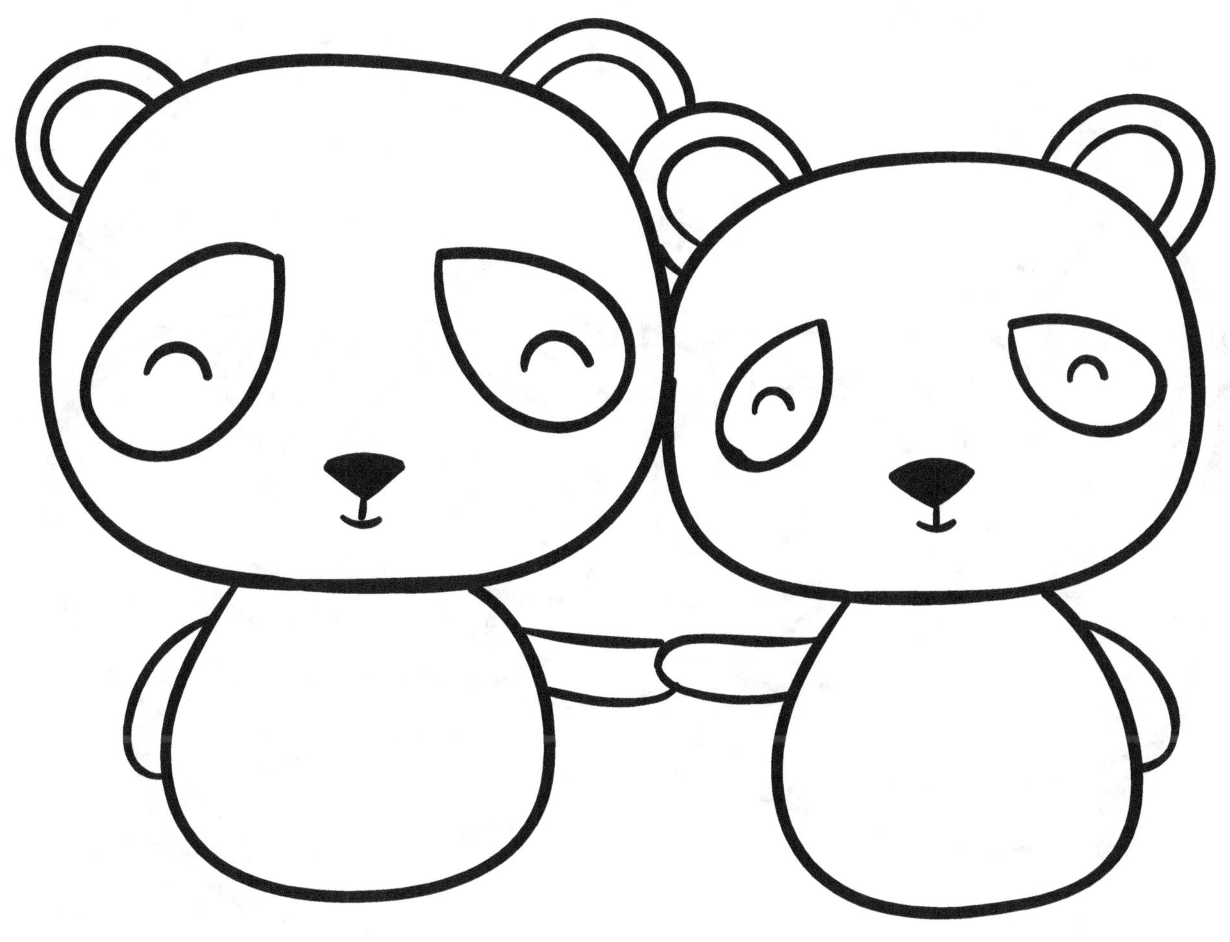

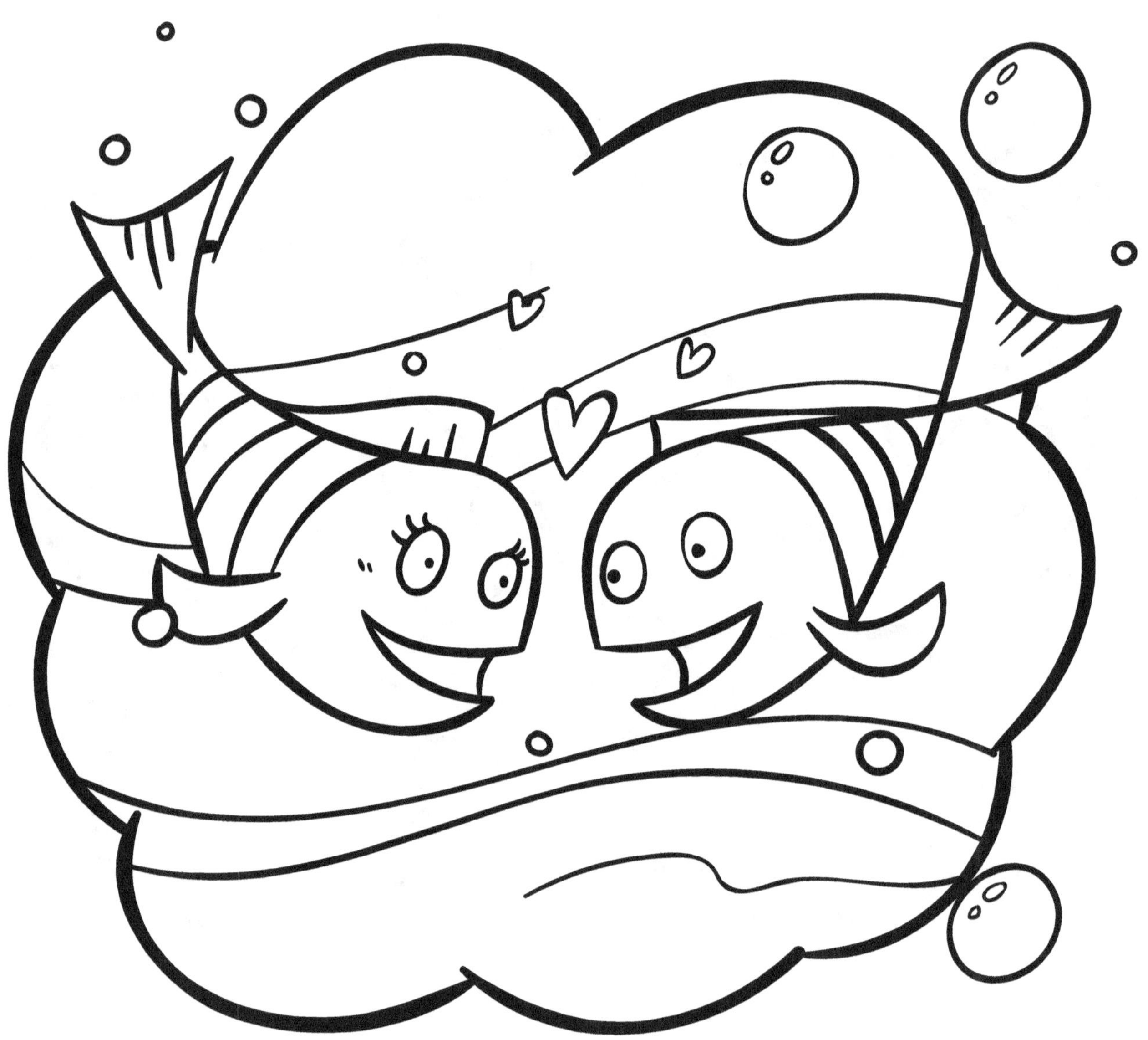

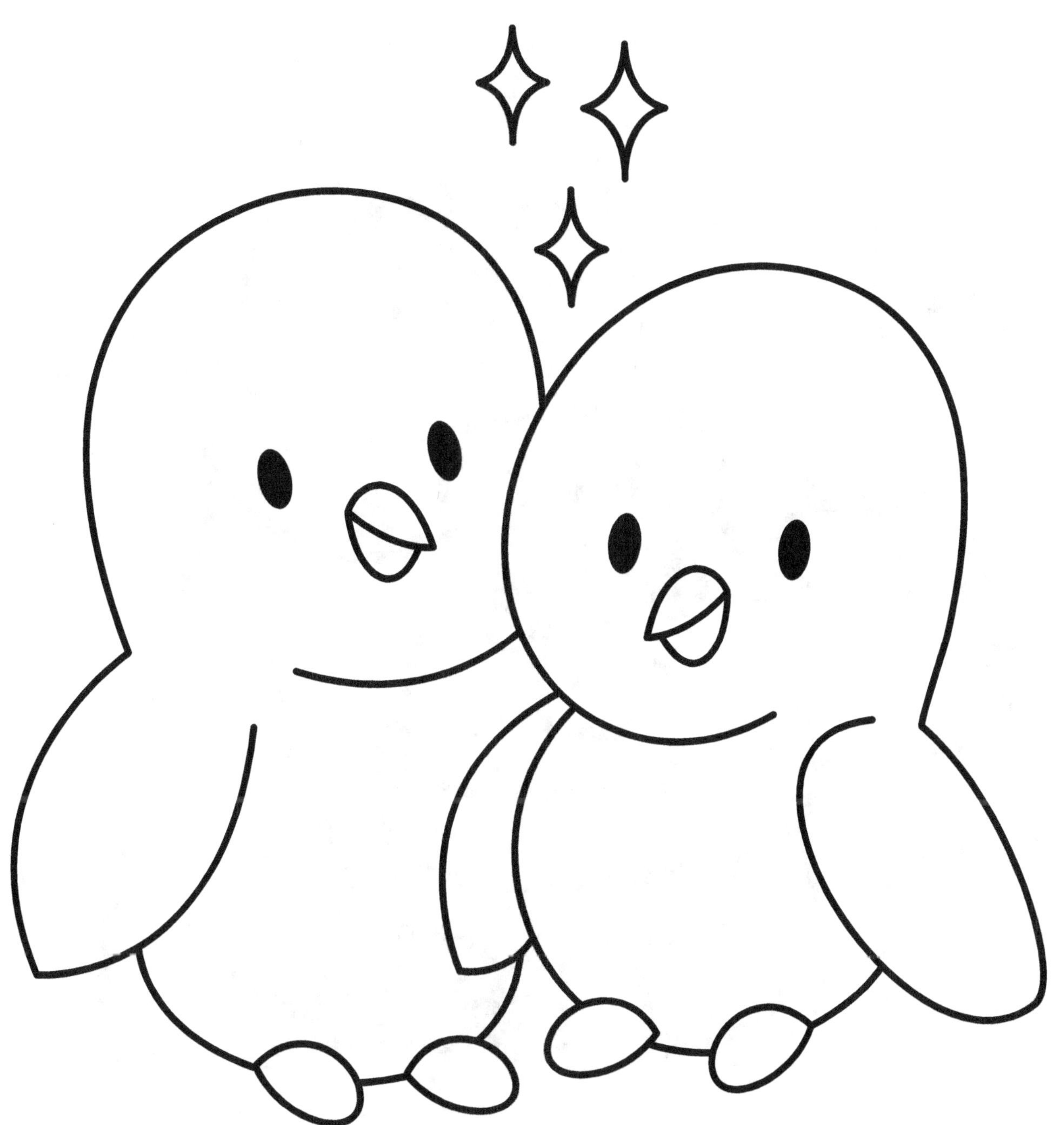

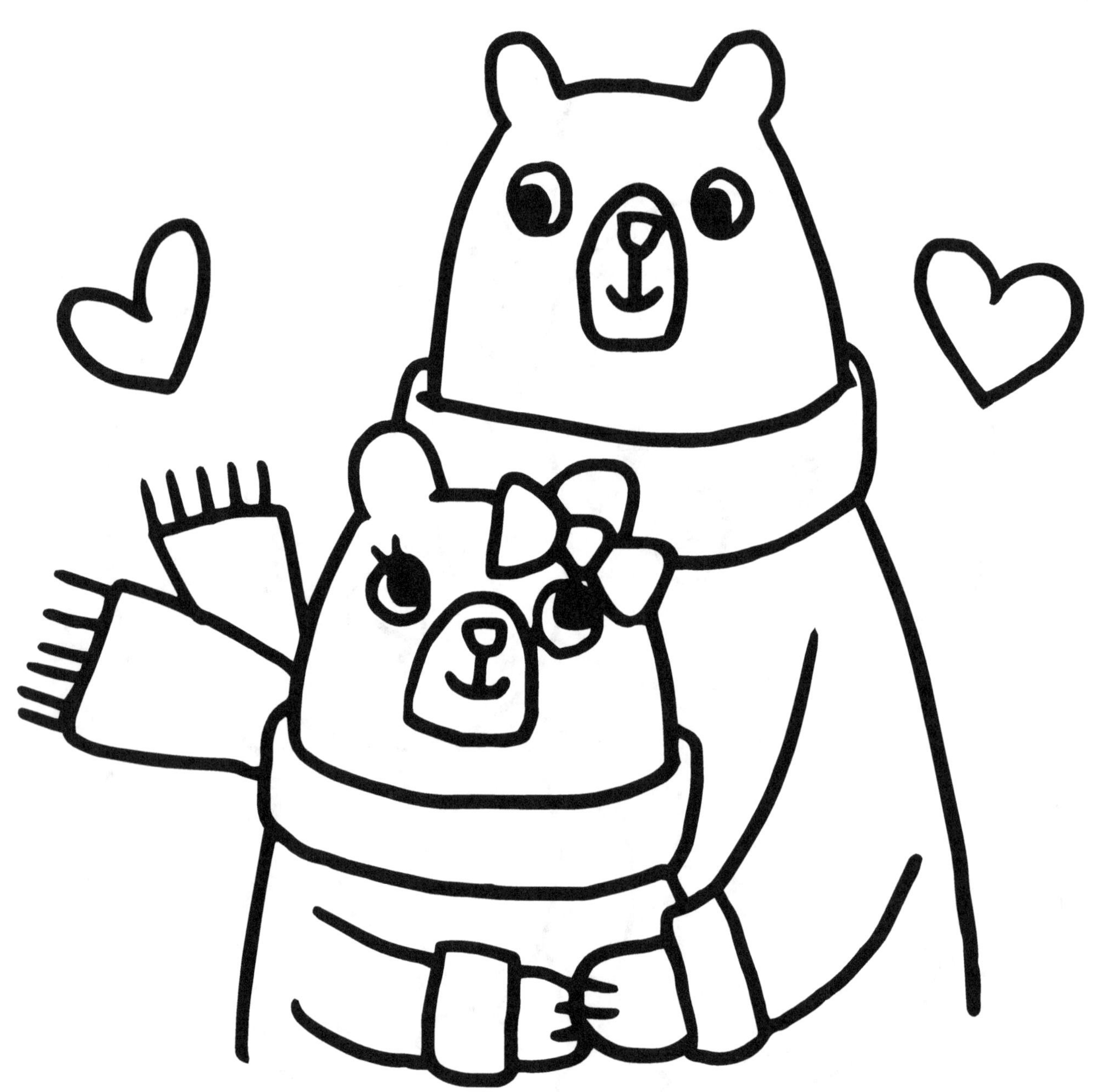

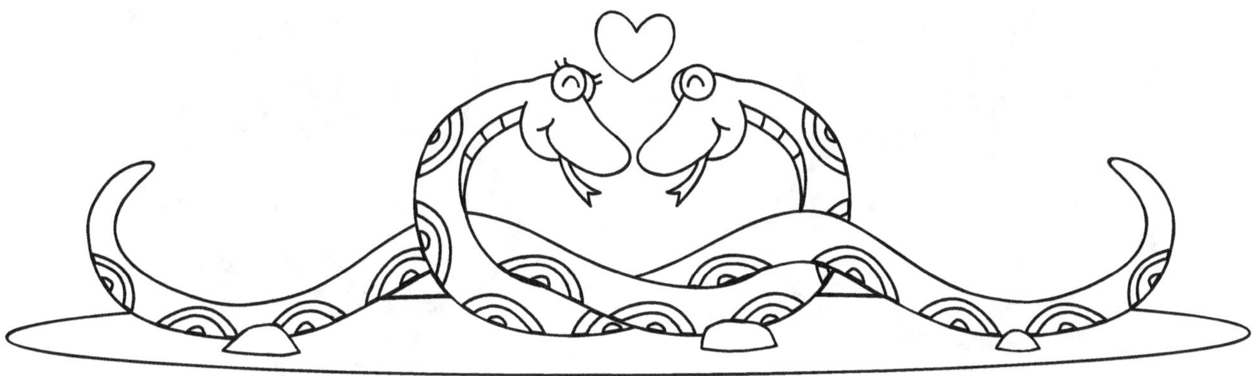

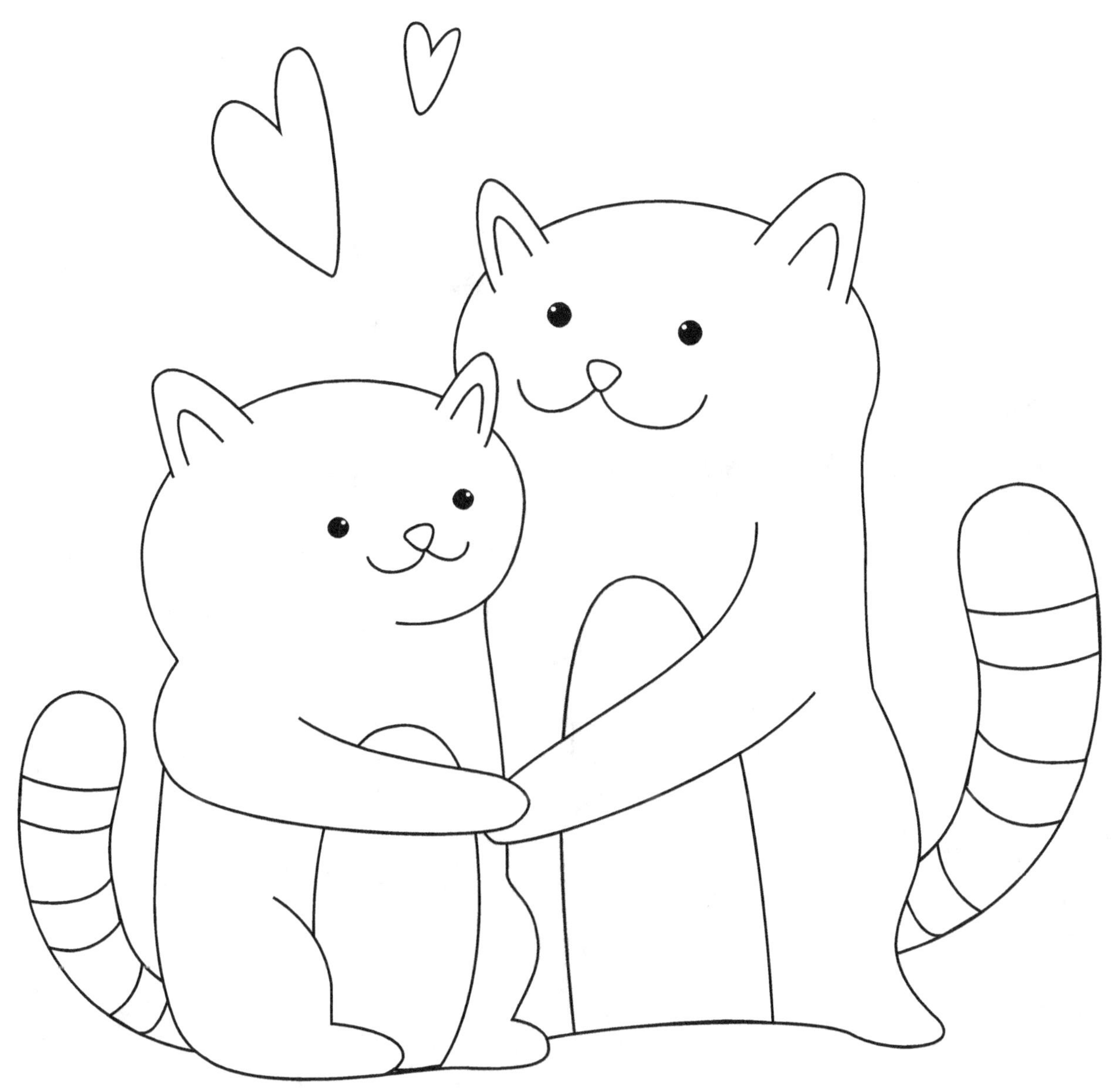

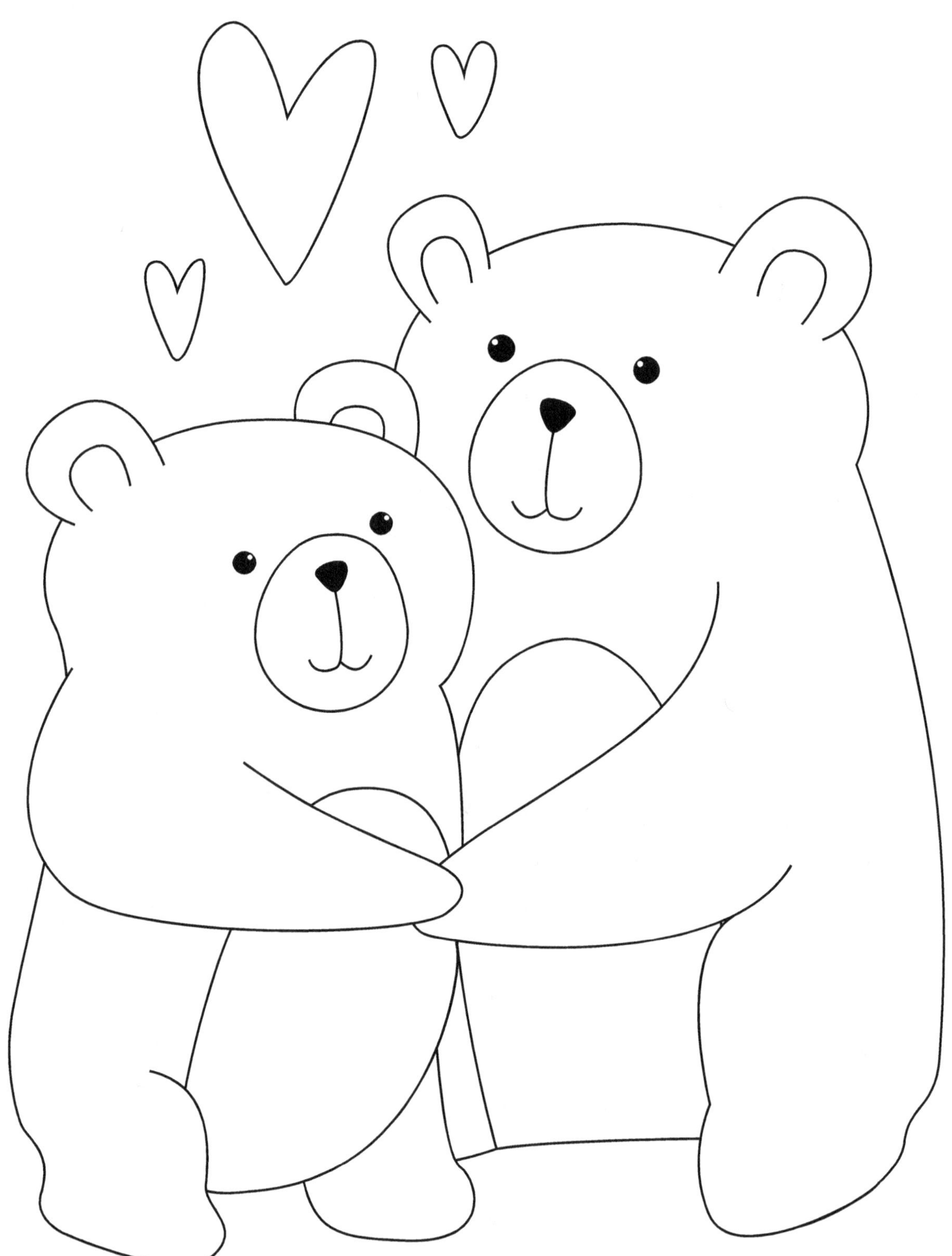

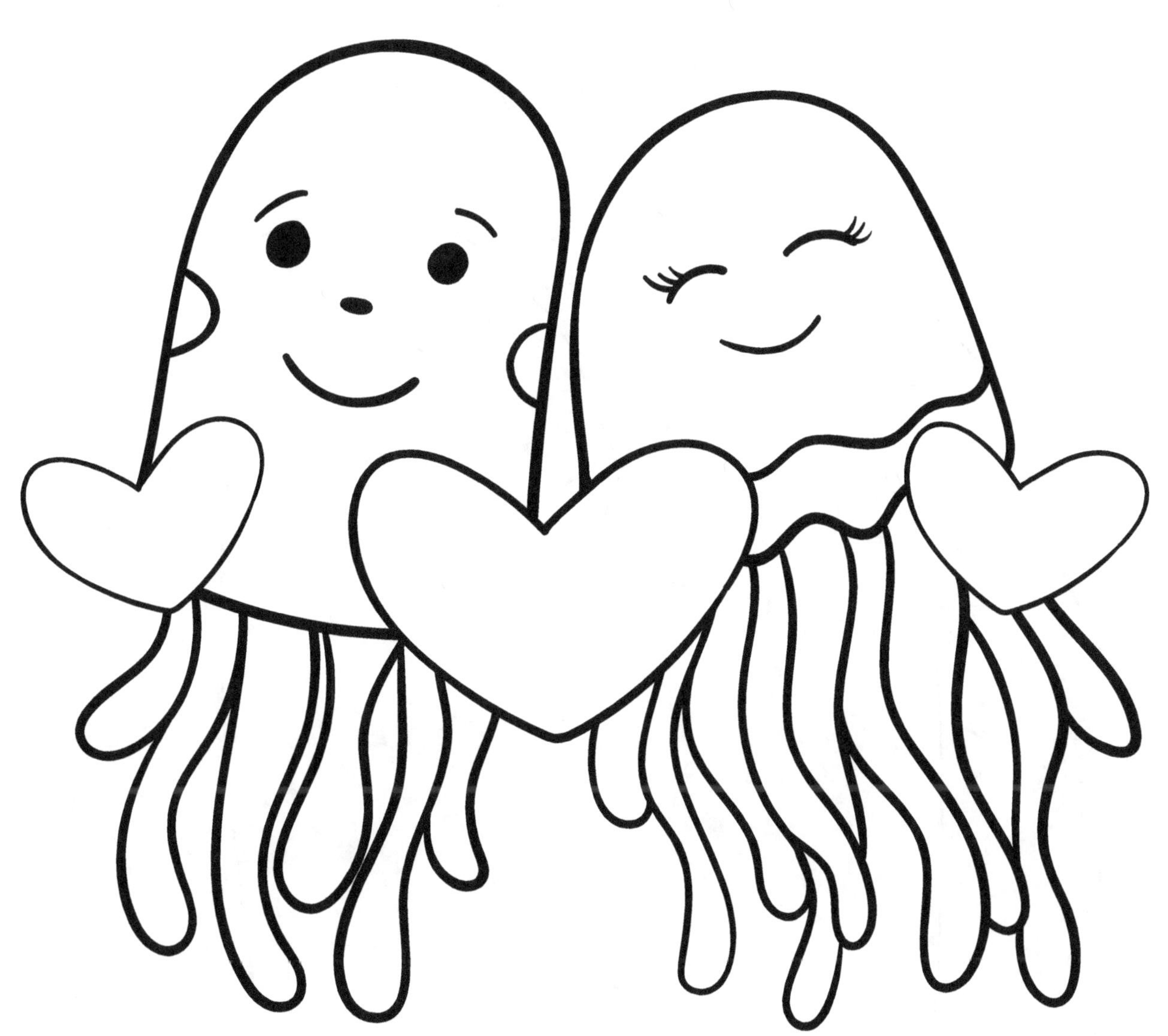

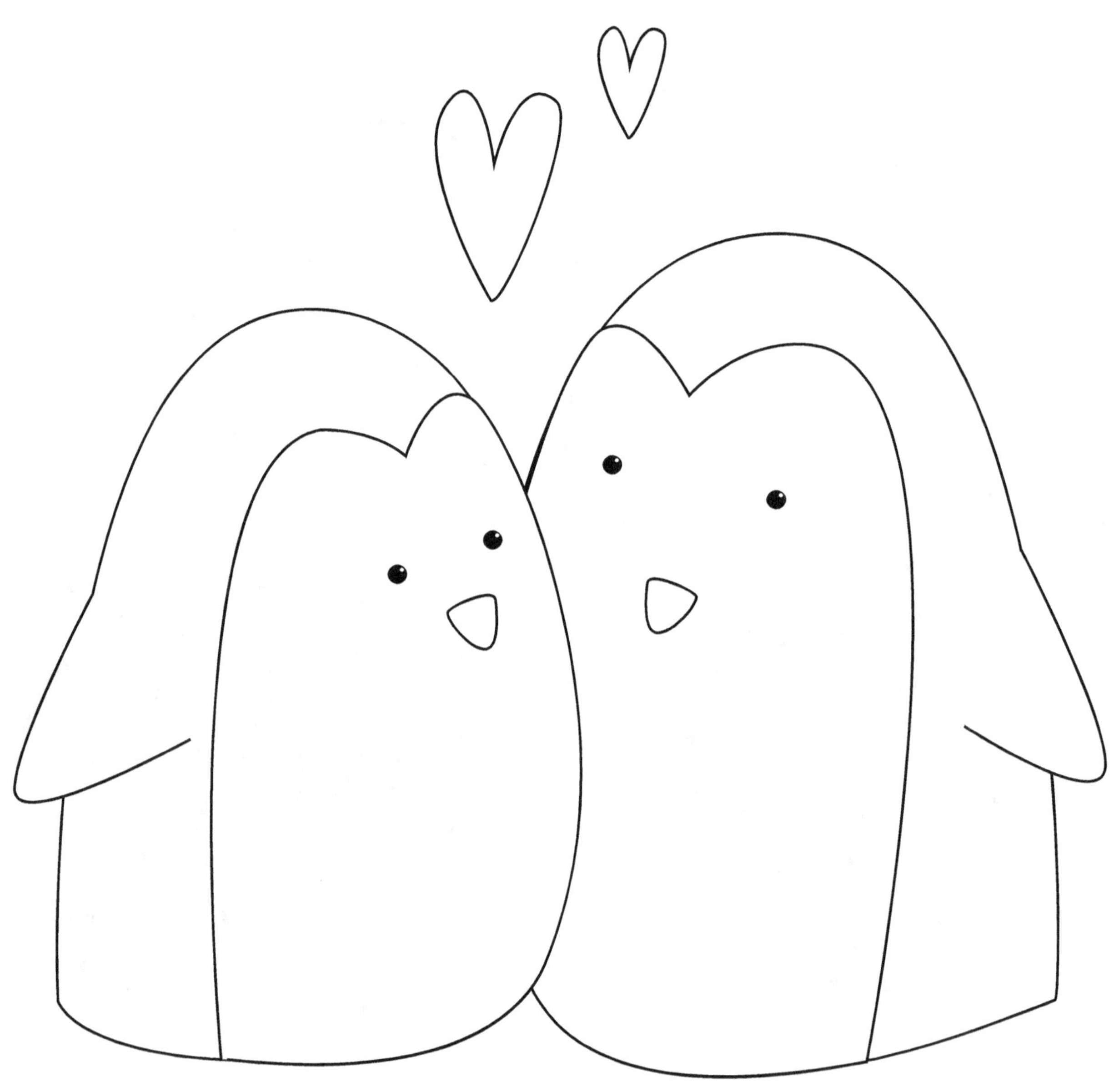

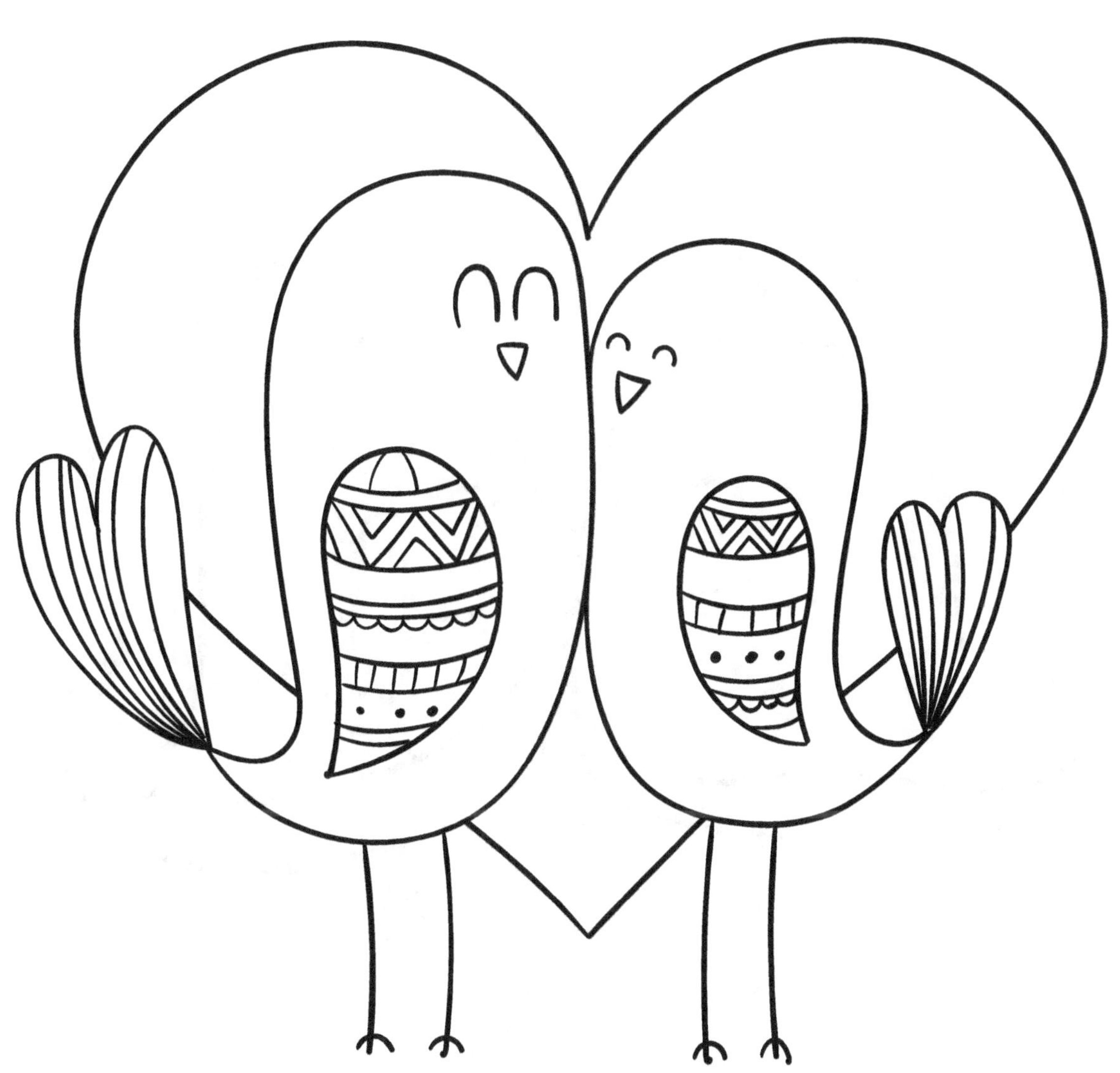

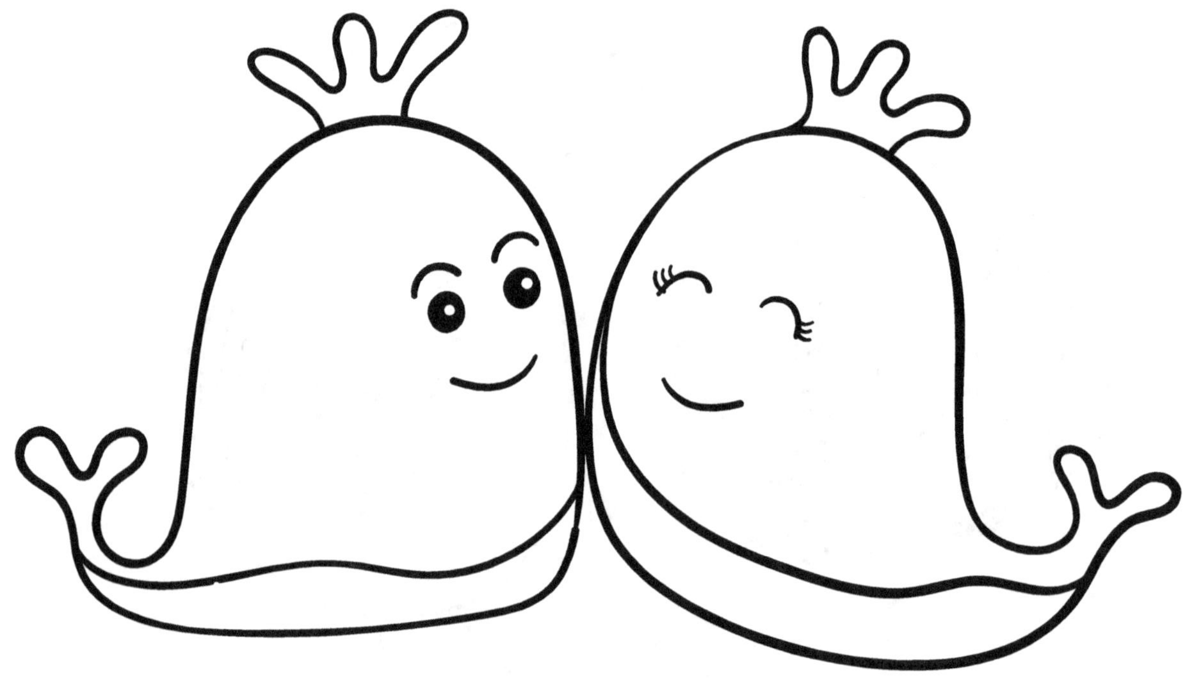

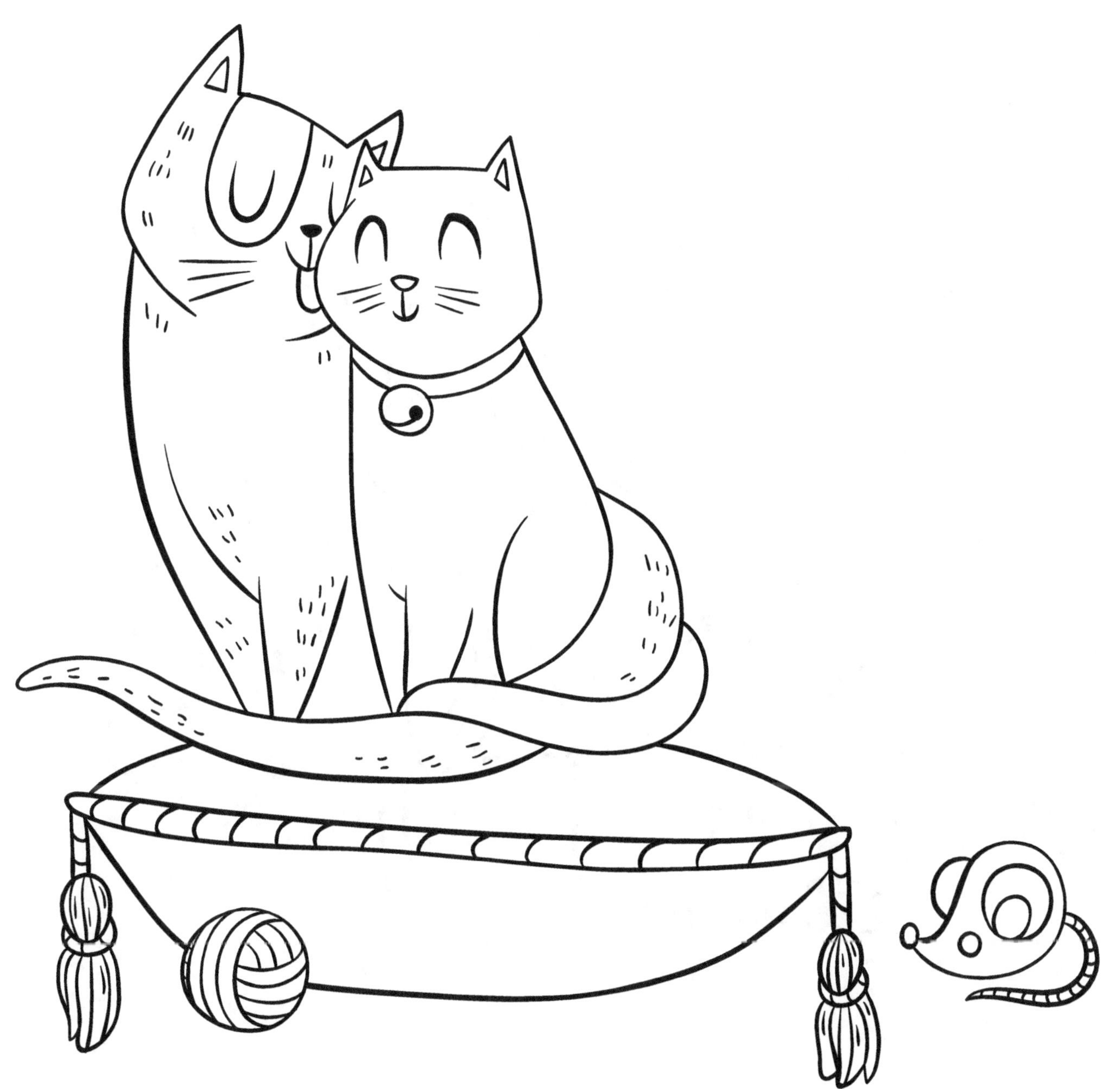

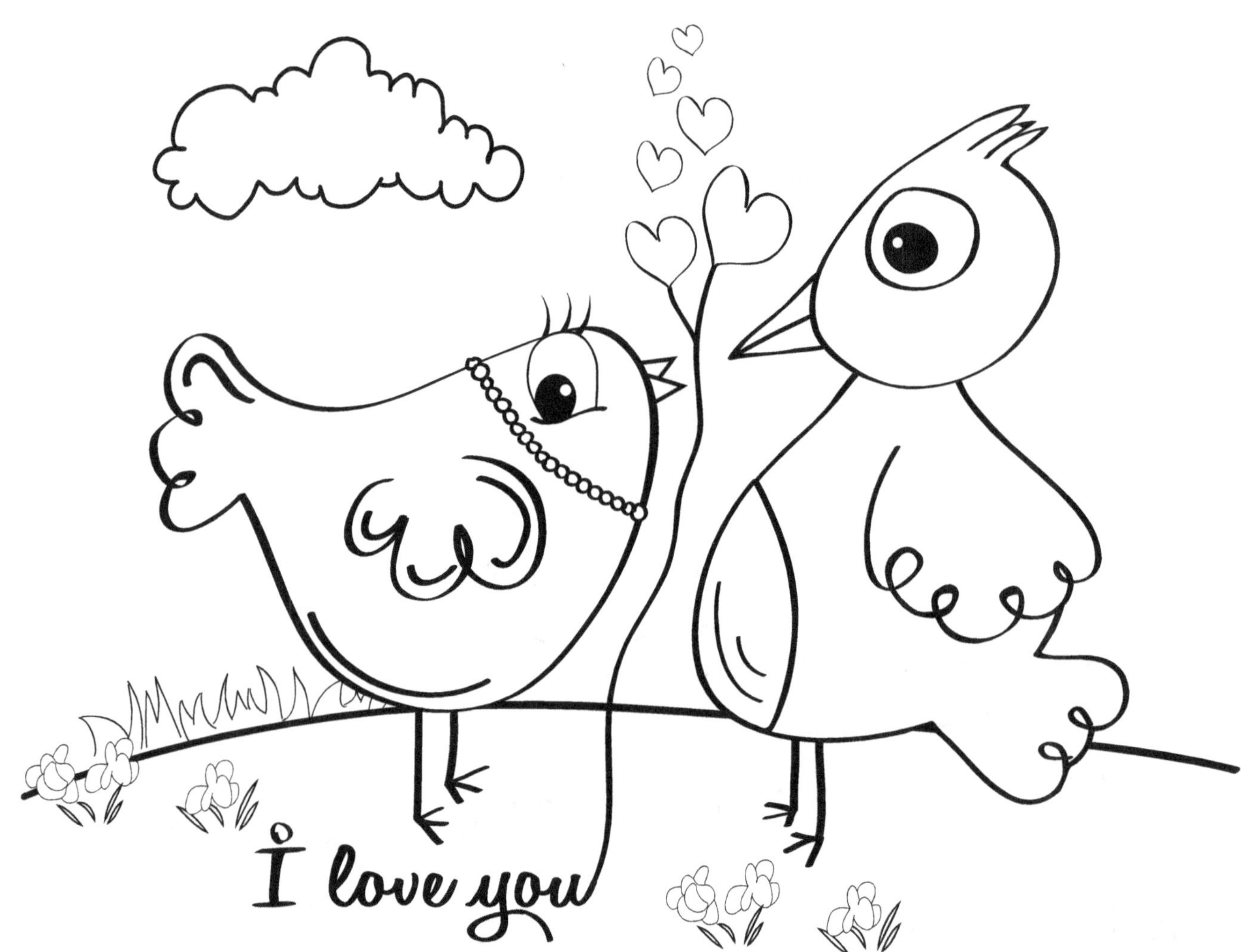
I love you

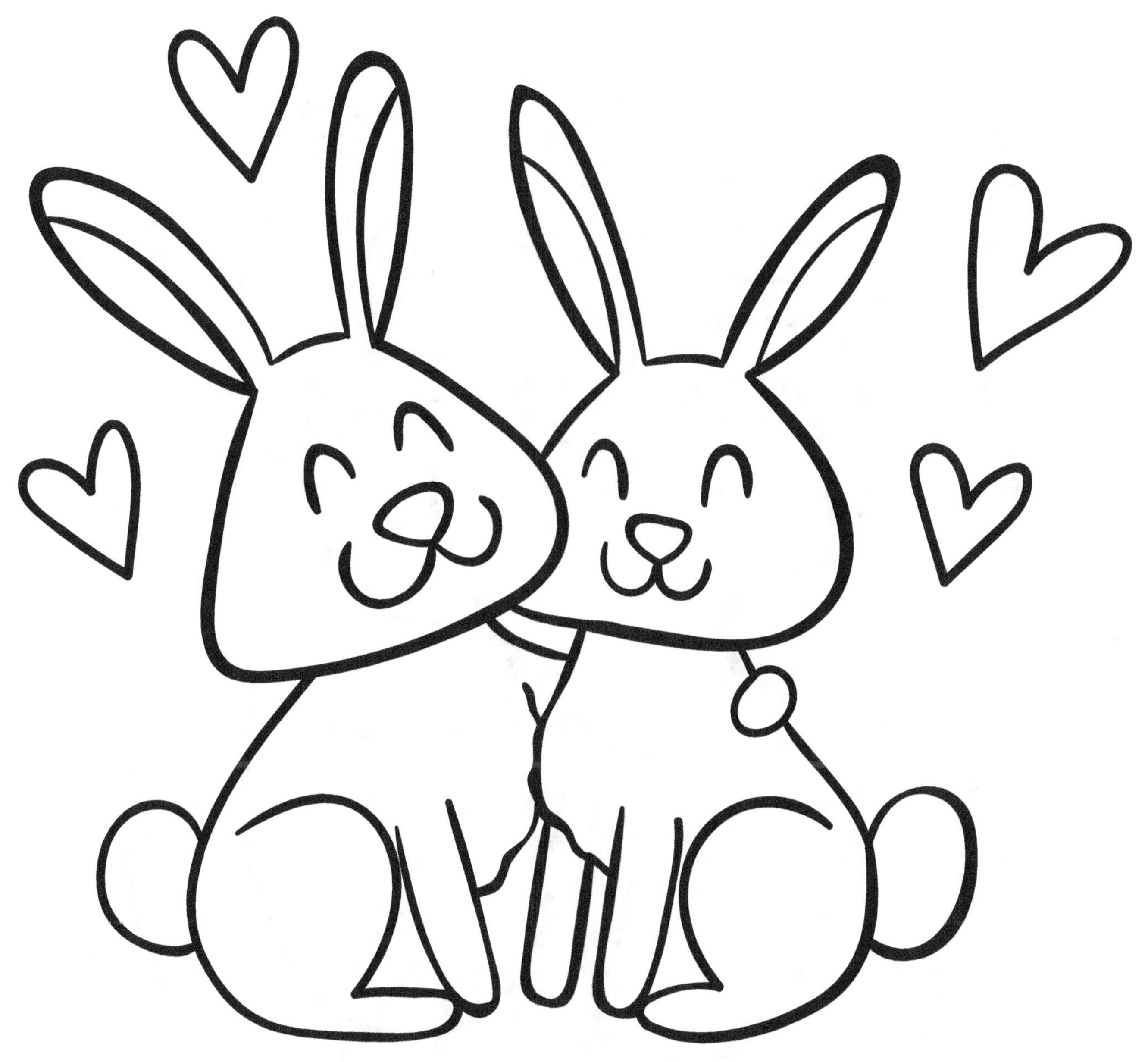

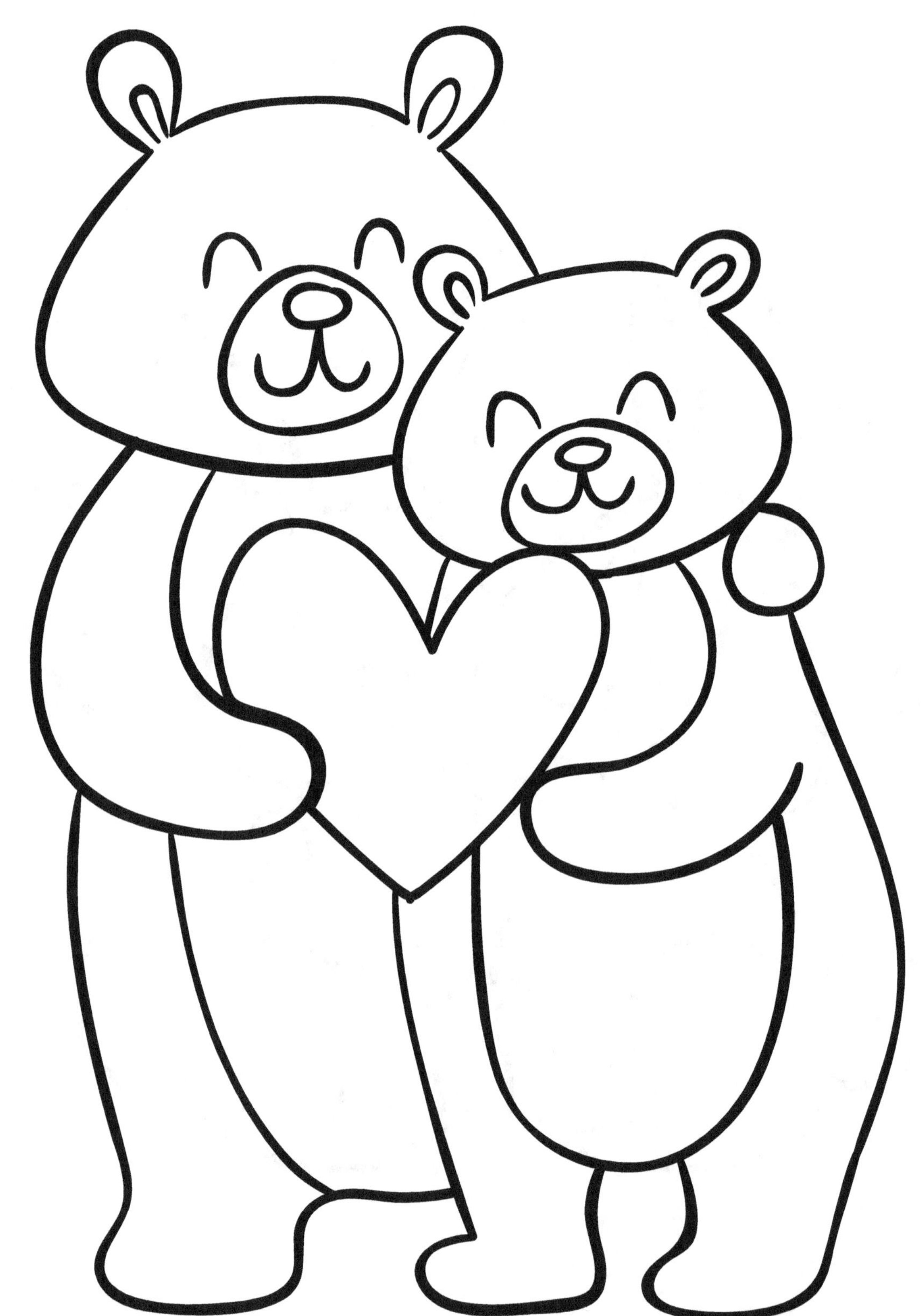

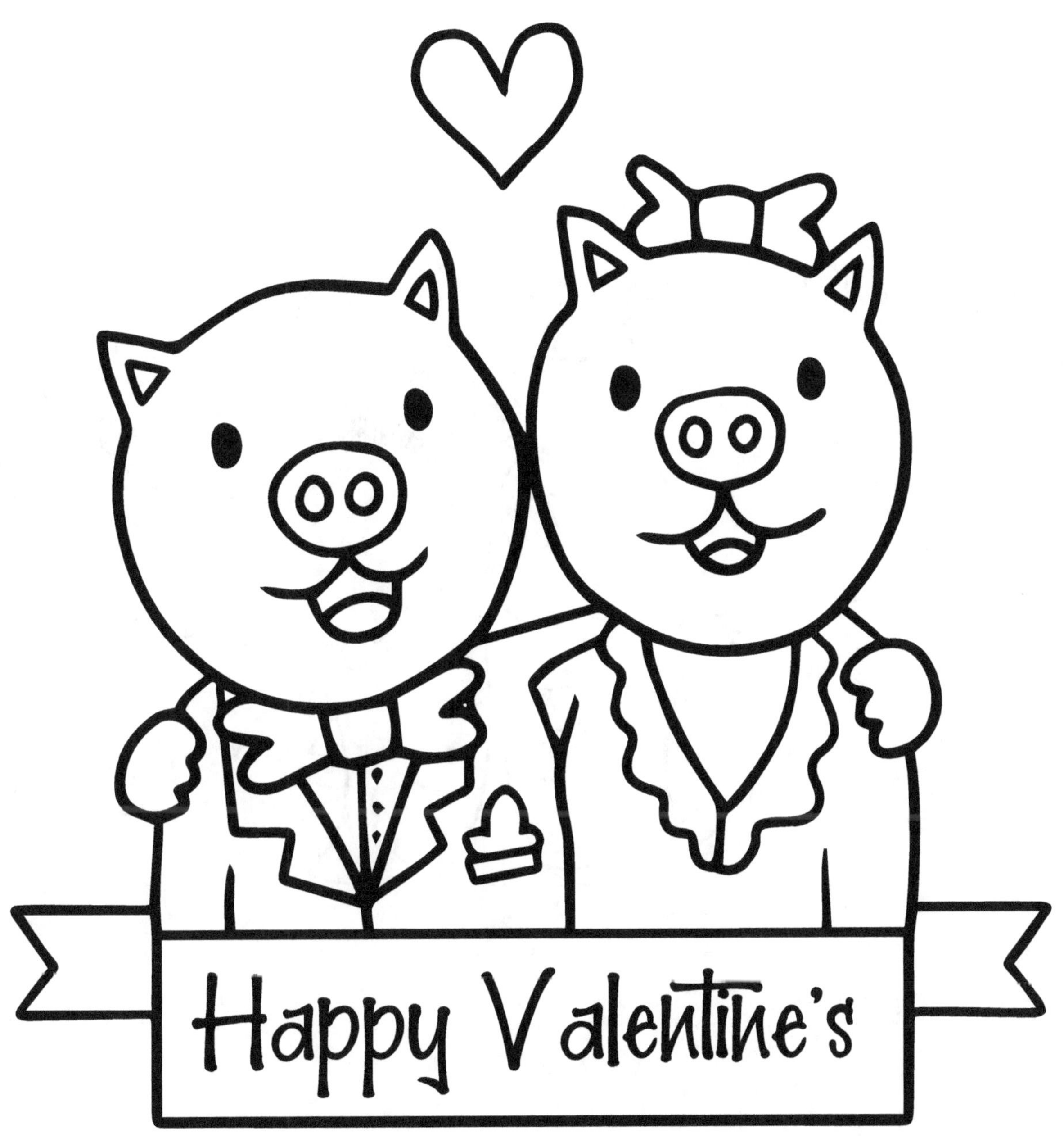

Happy Valentine's

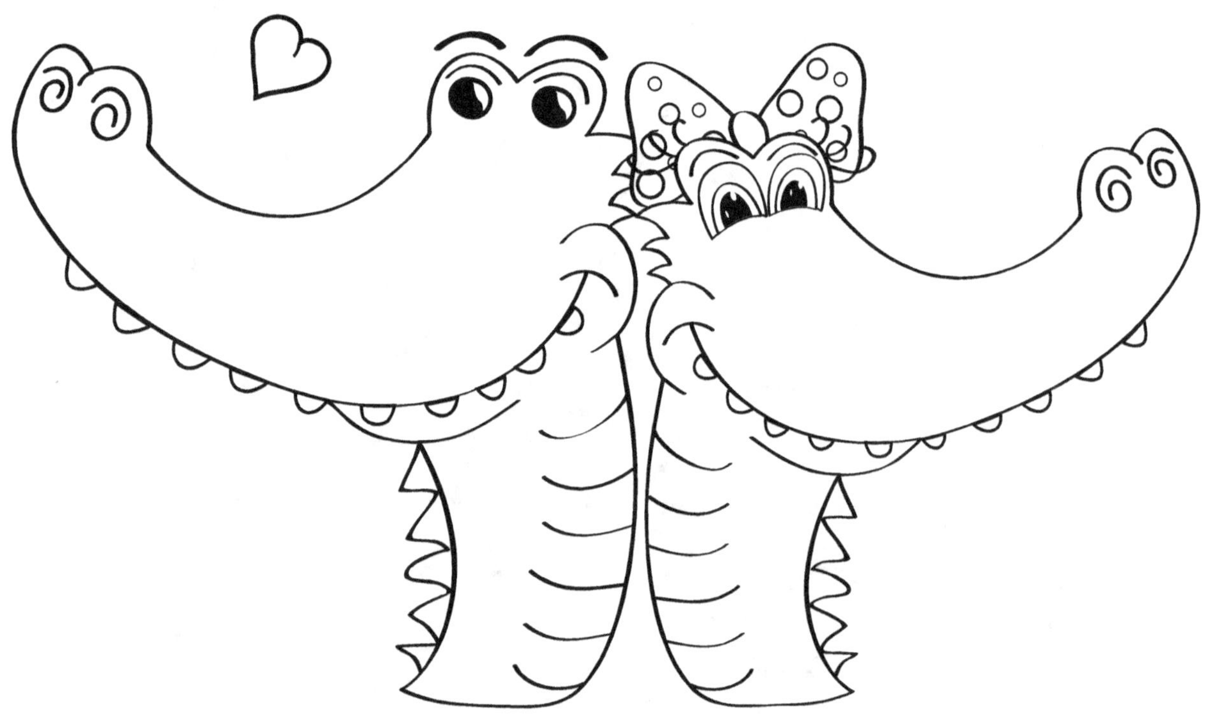

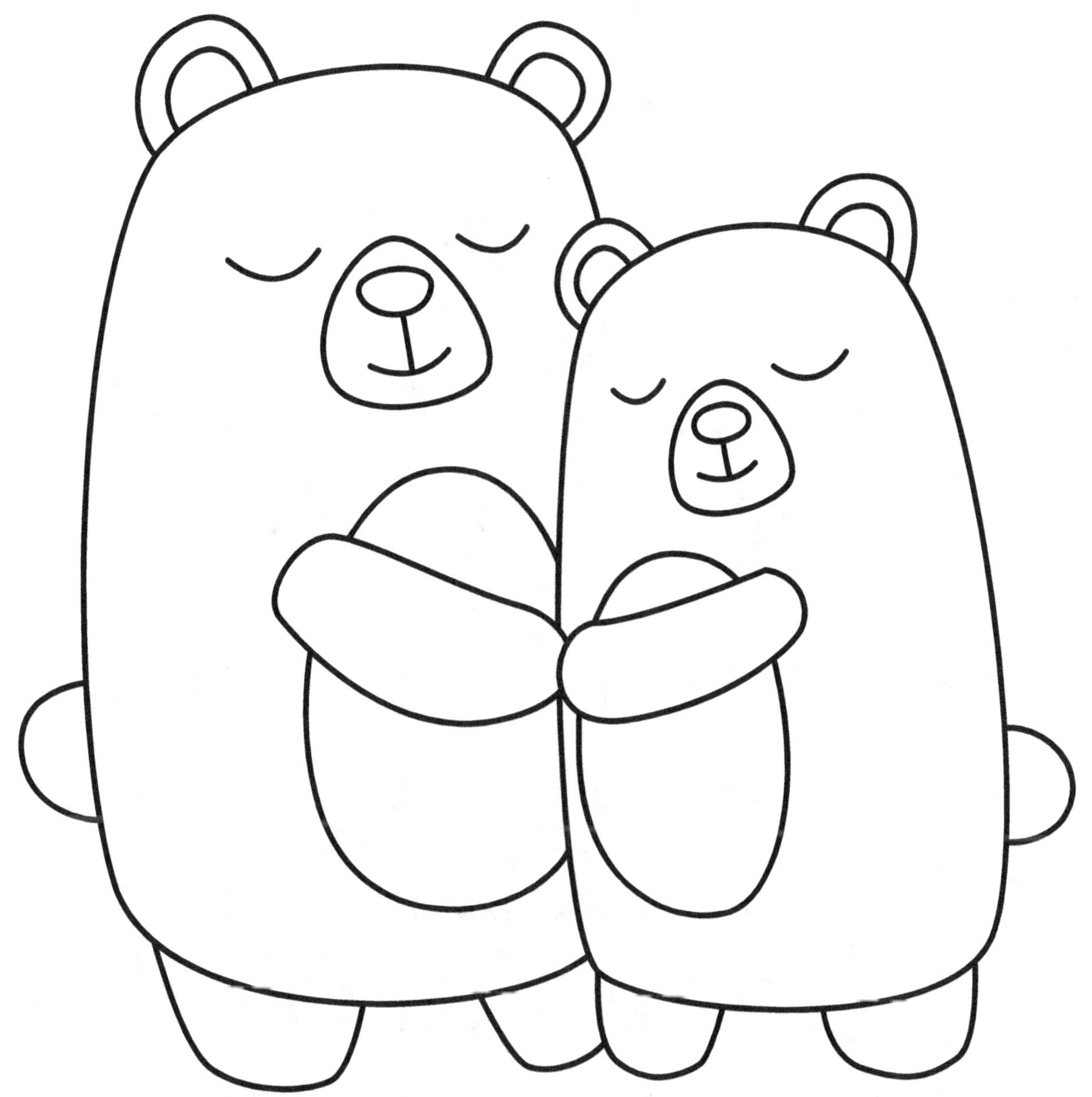

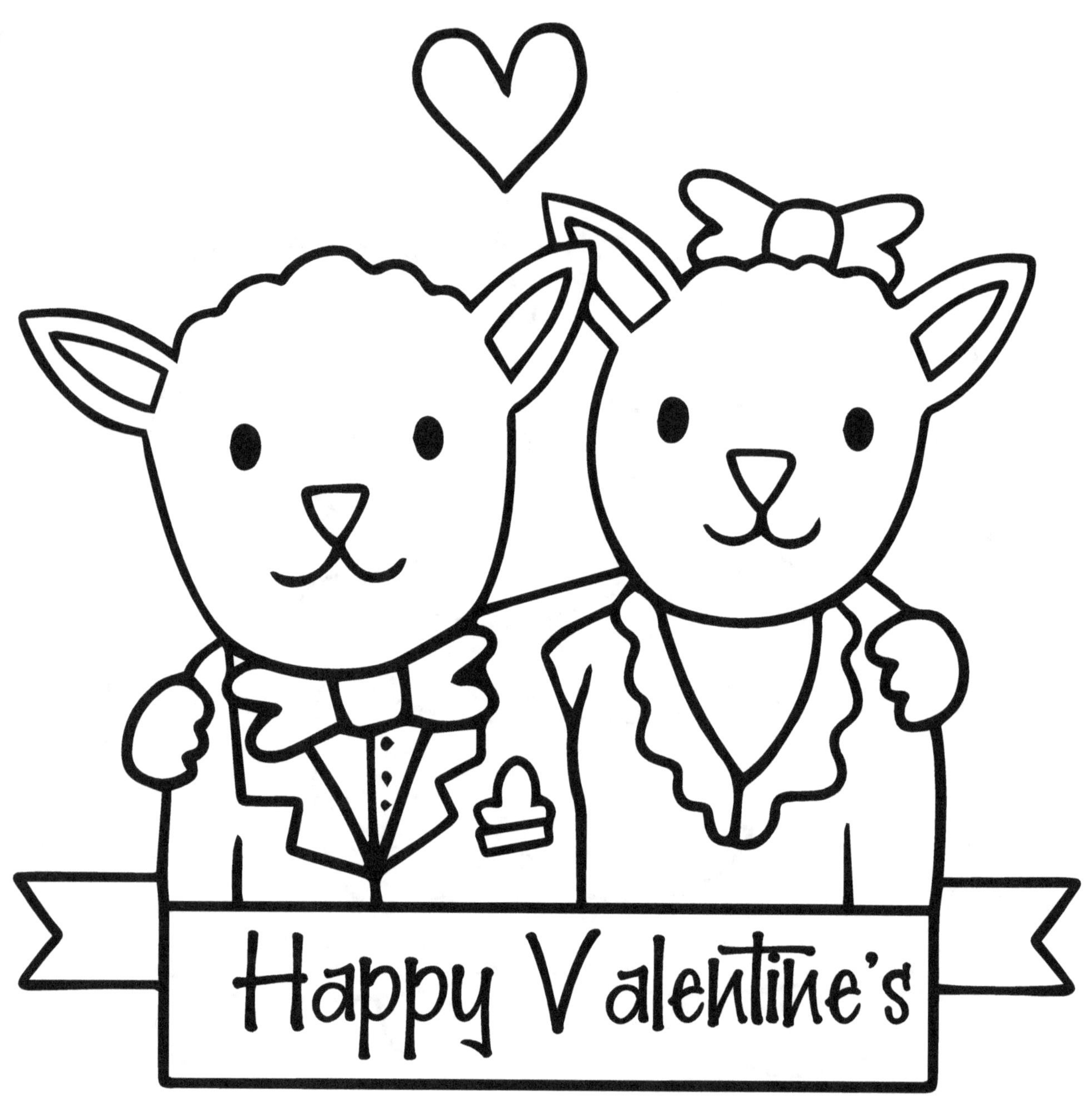
Happy Valentine's

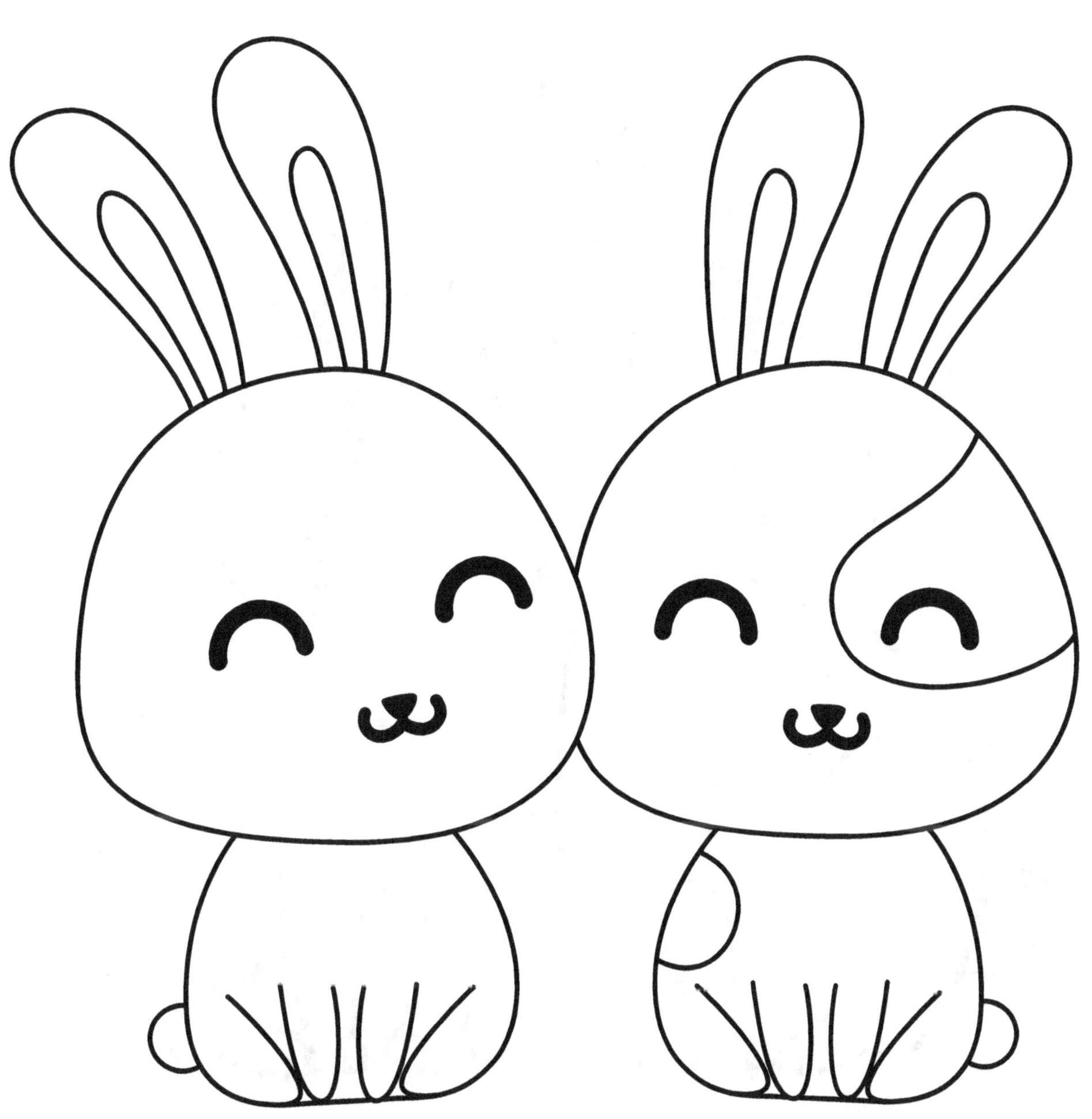

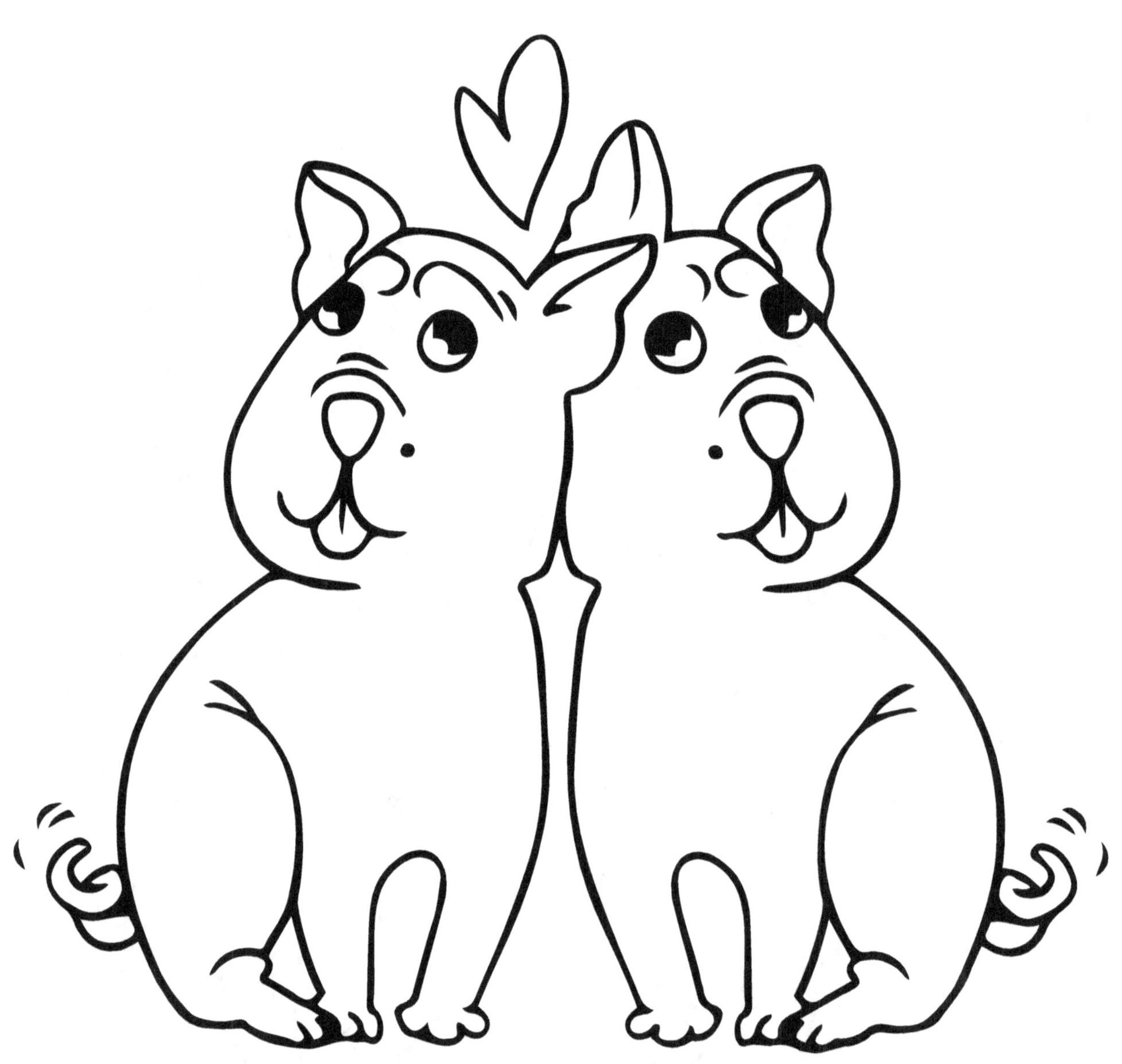

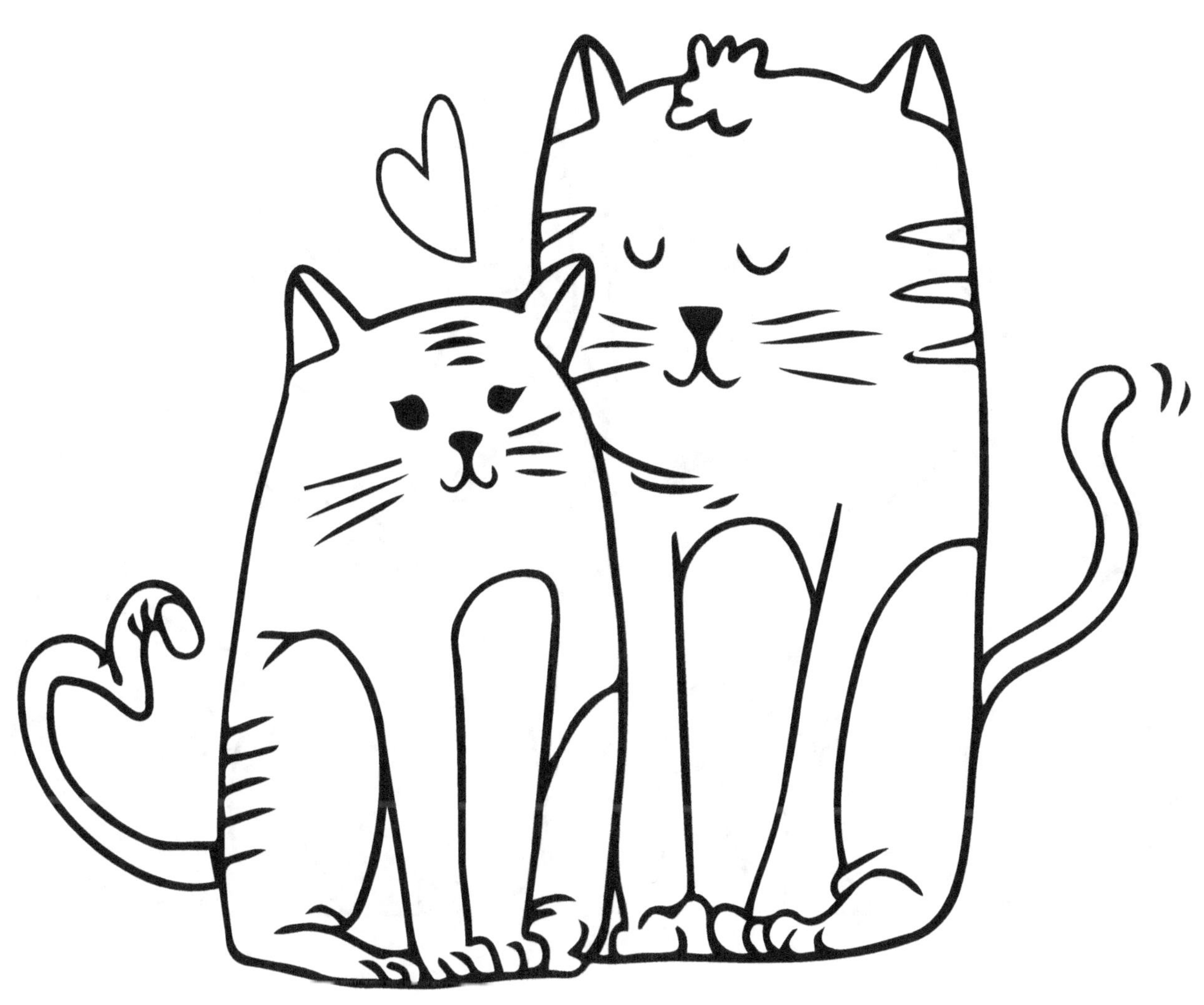

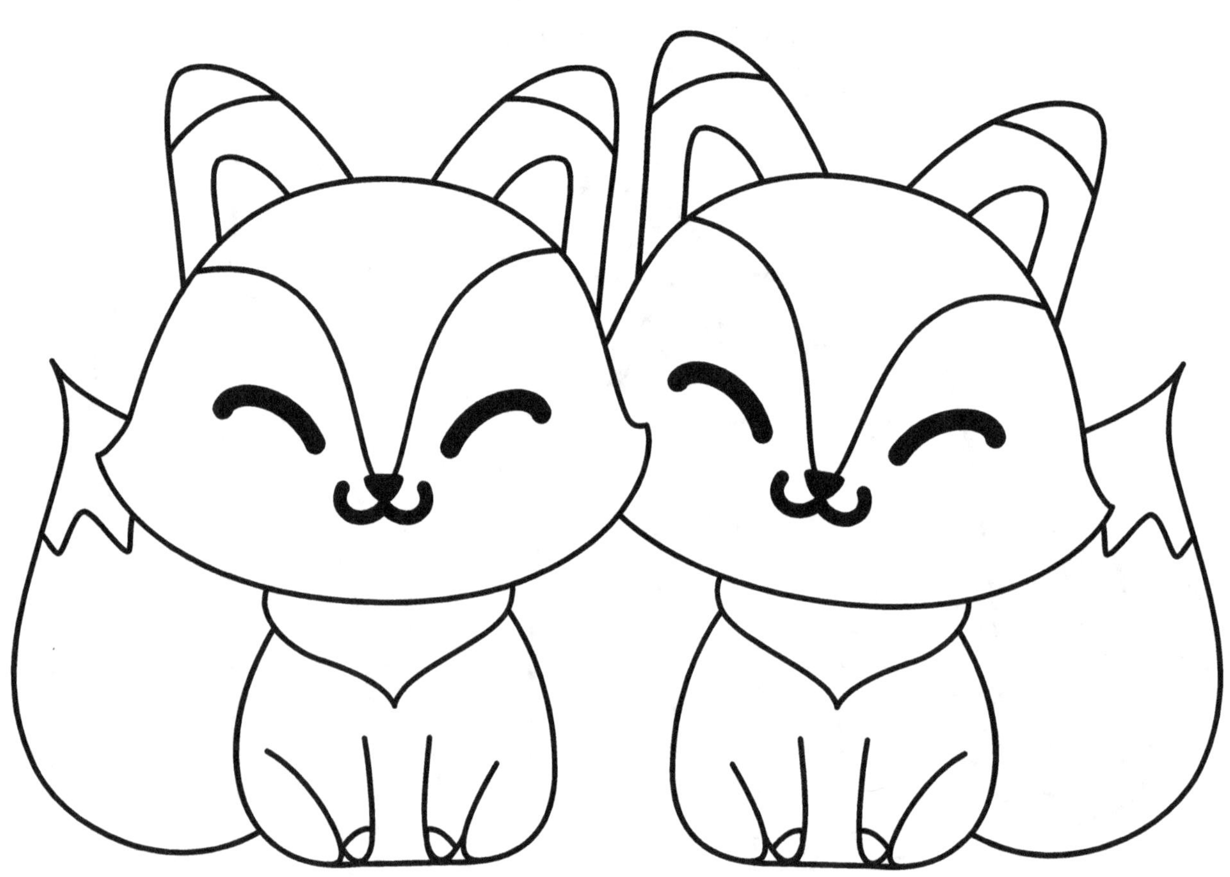

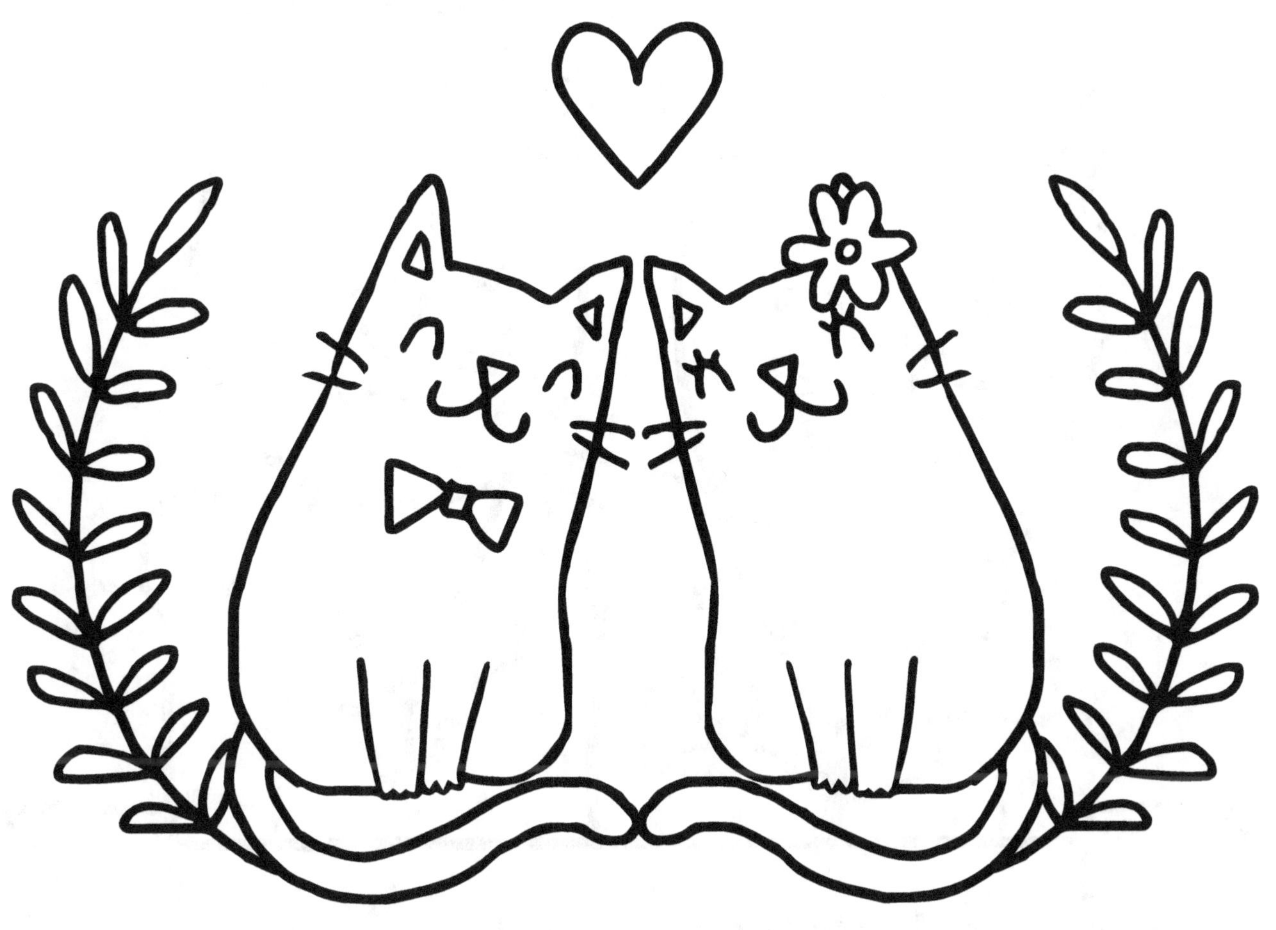

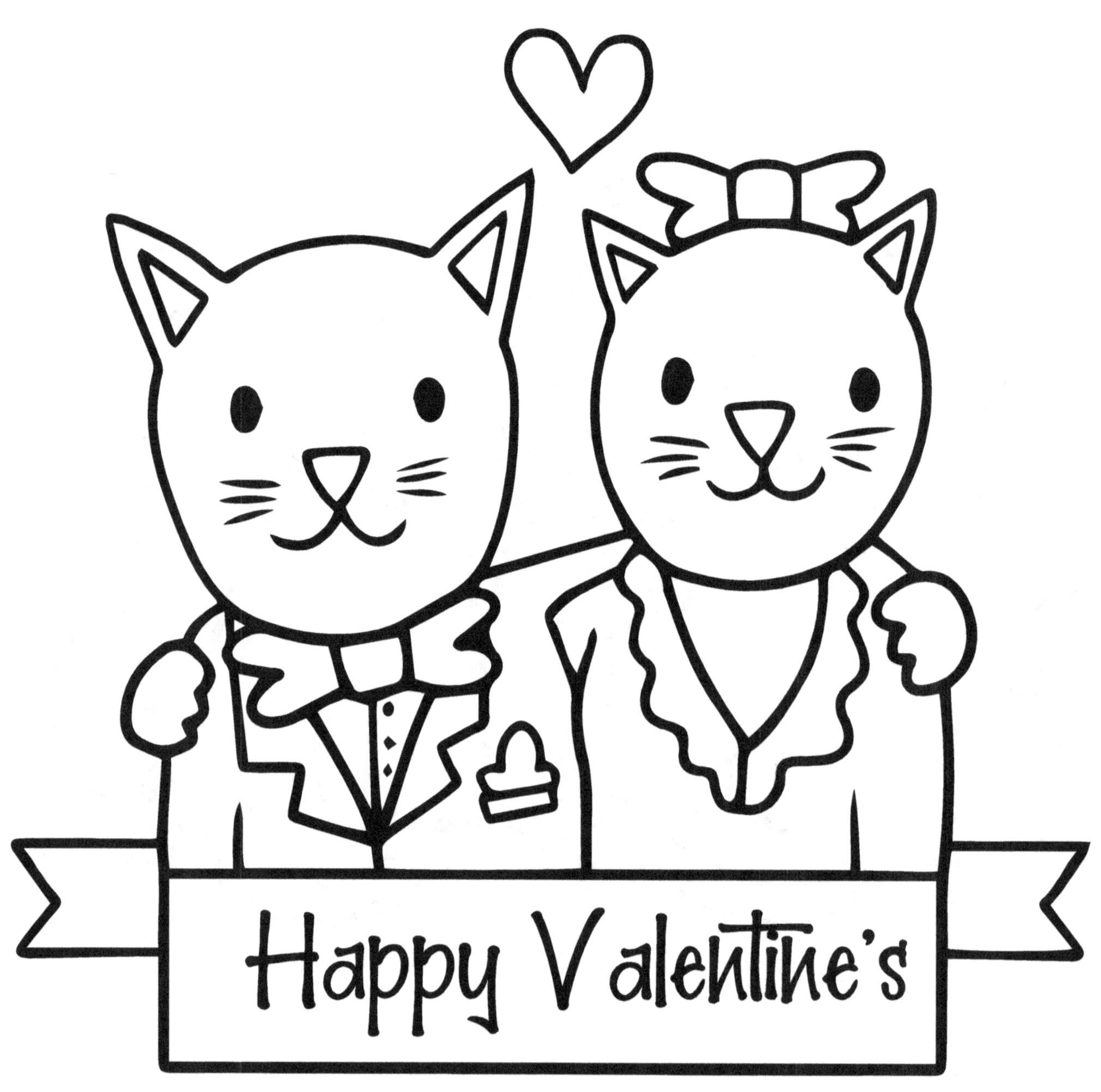
Happy Valentine's

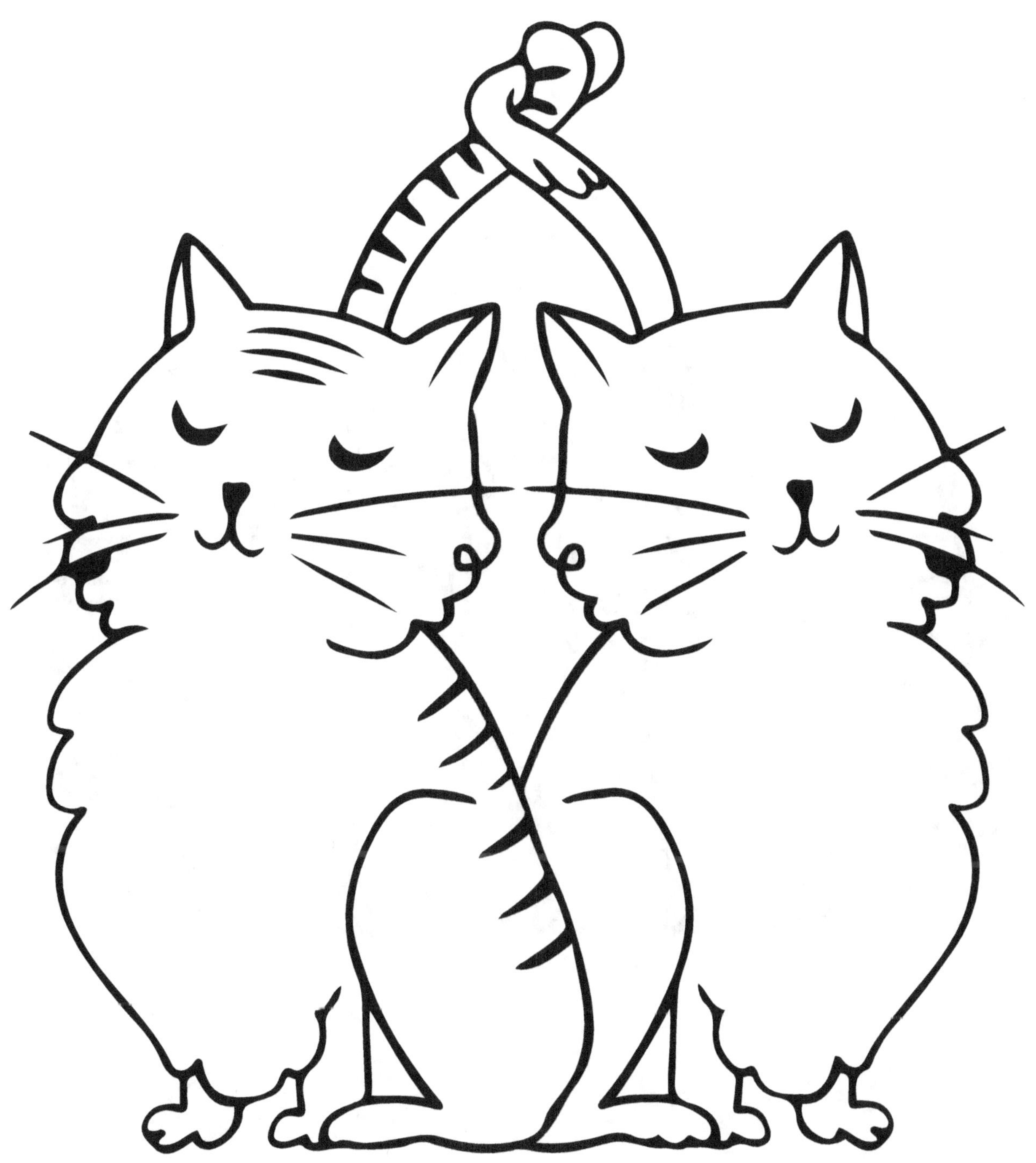

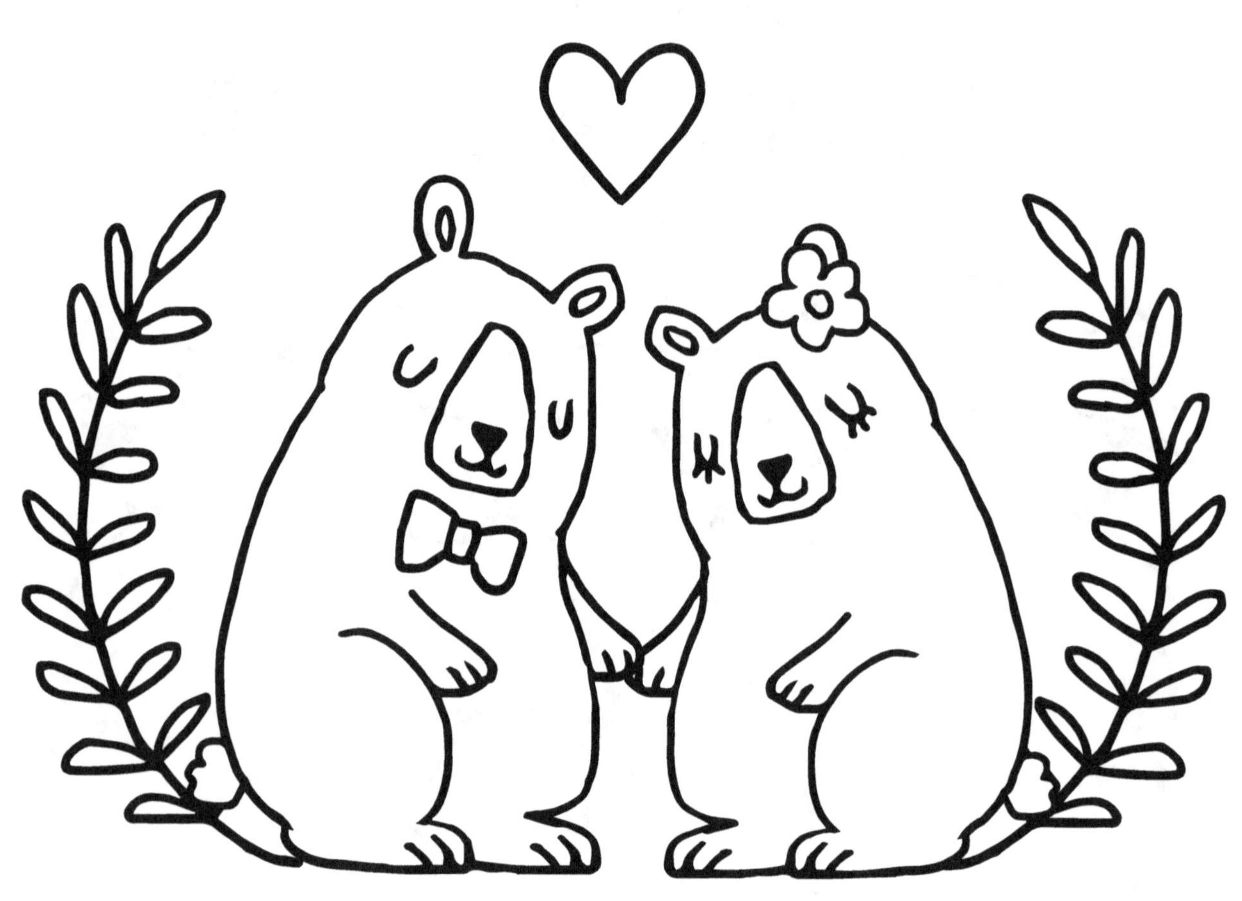

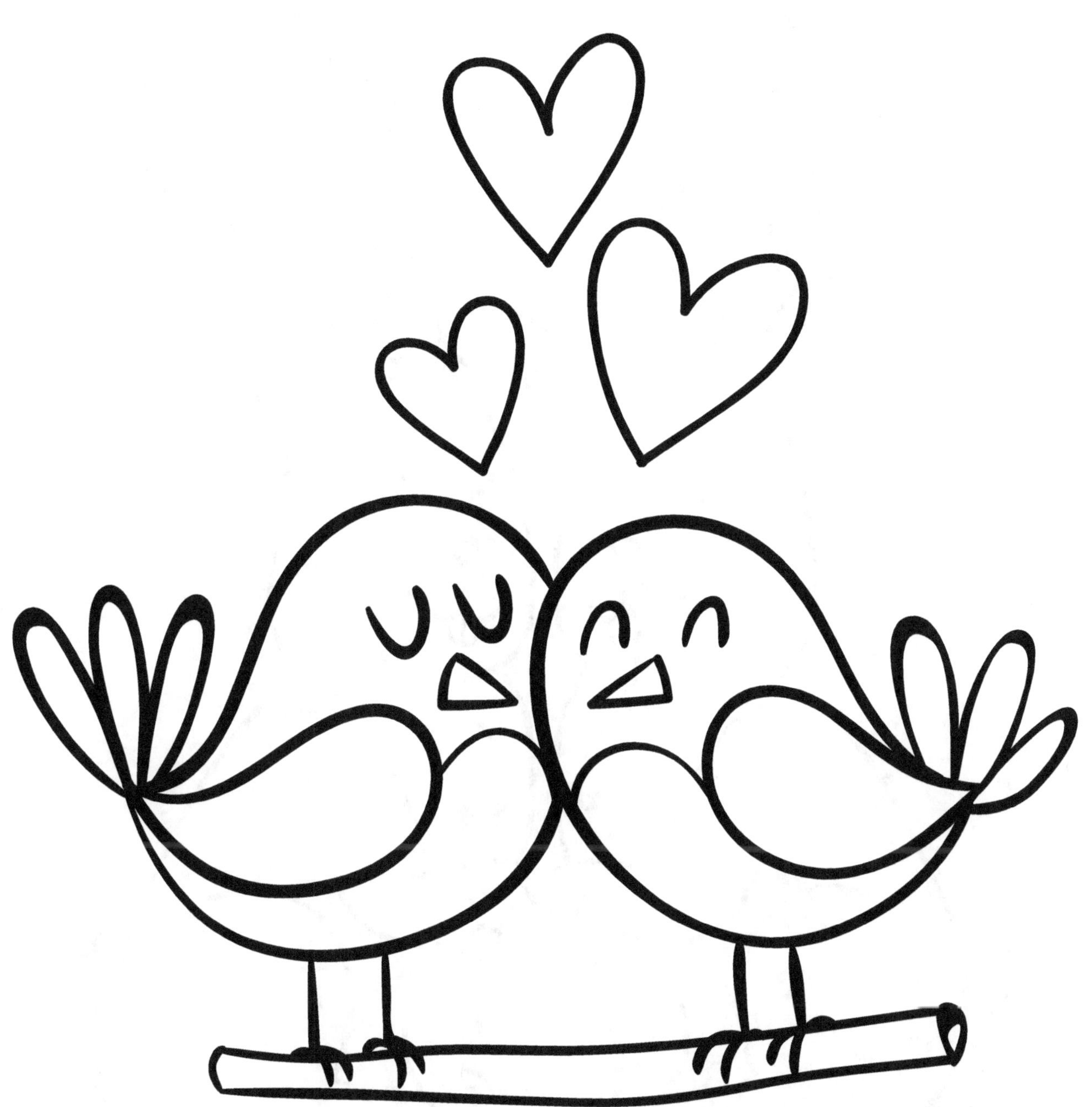

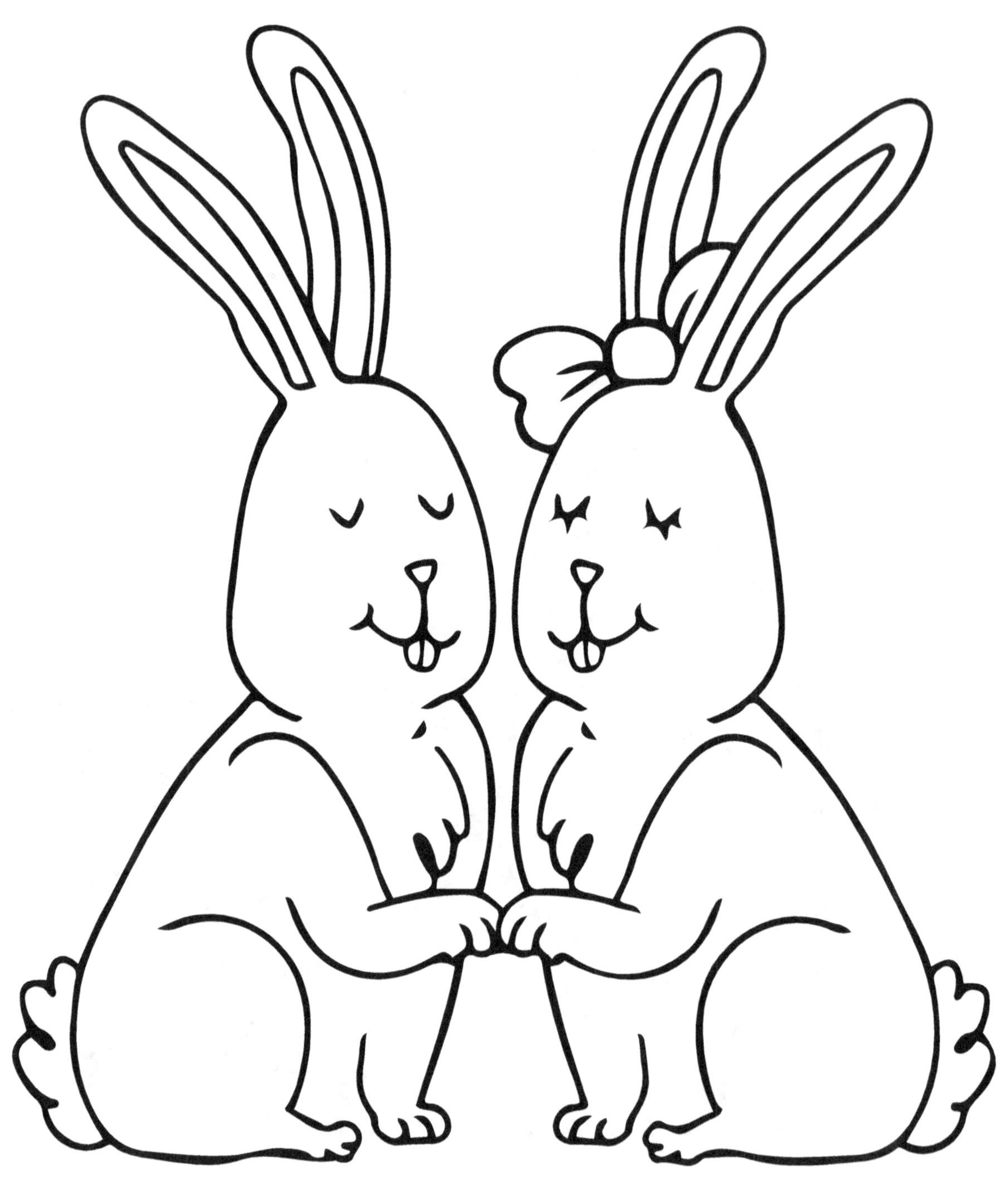

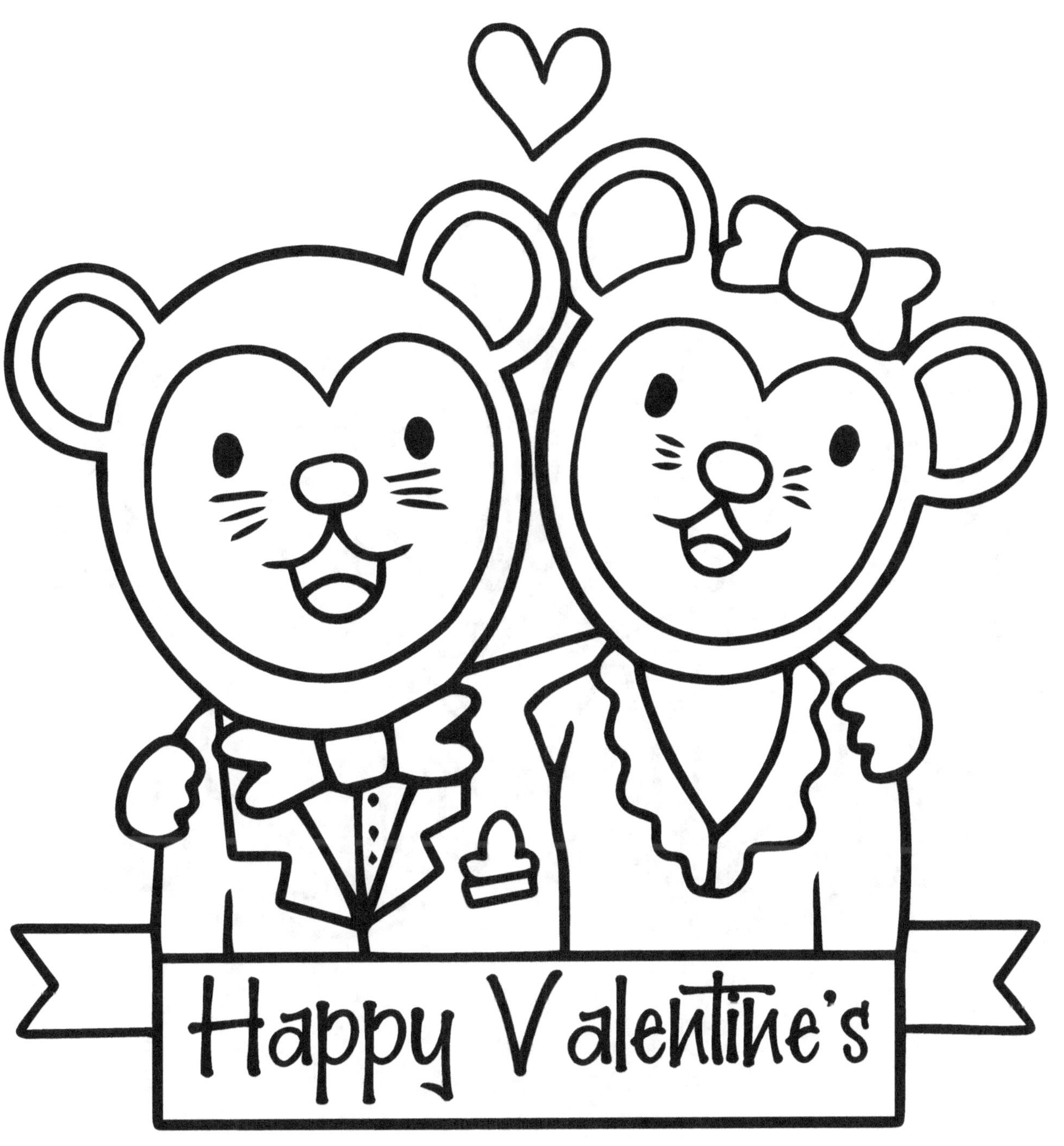
Happy Valentine's

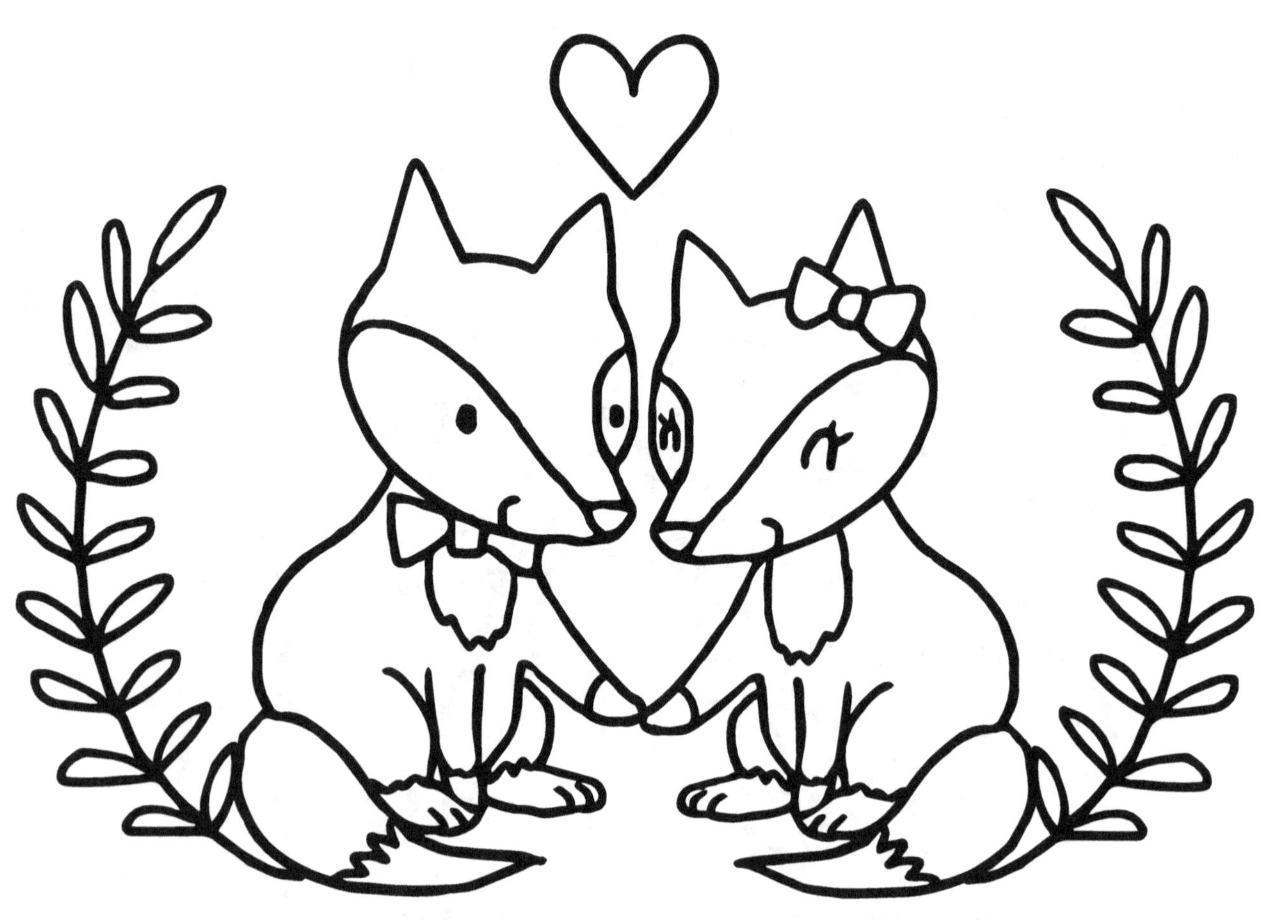

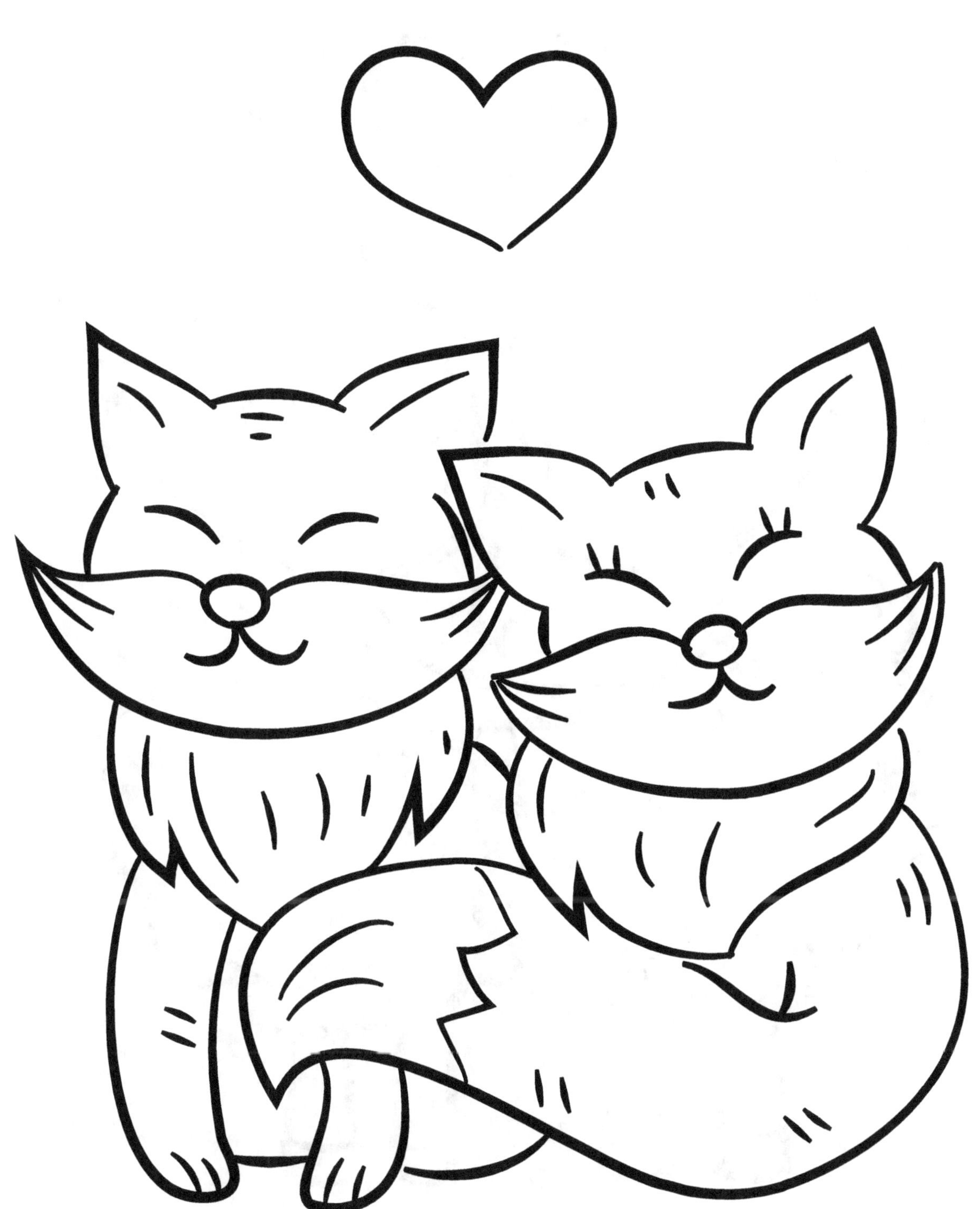

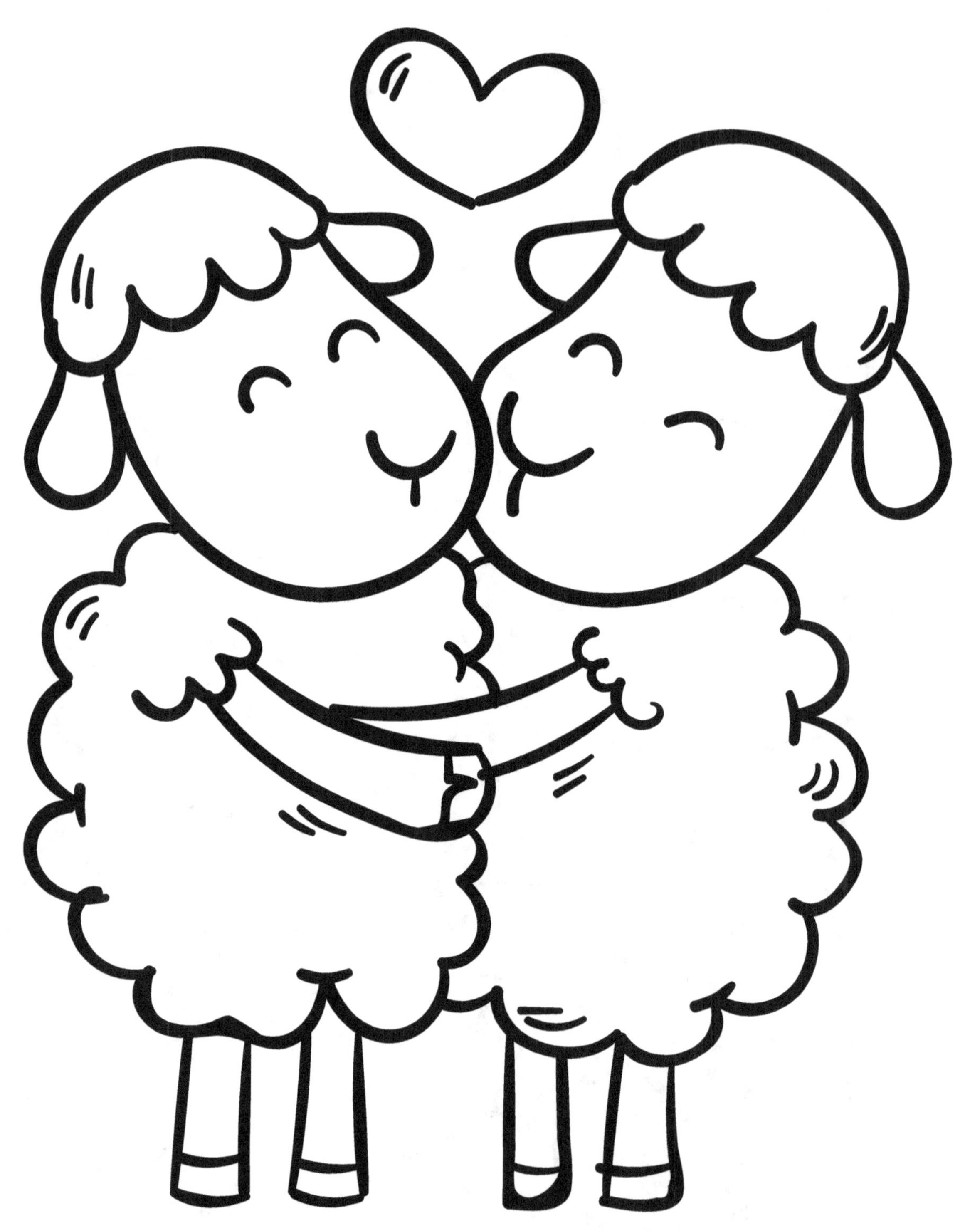

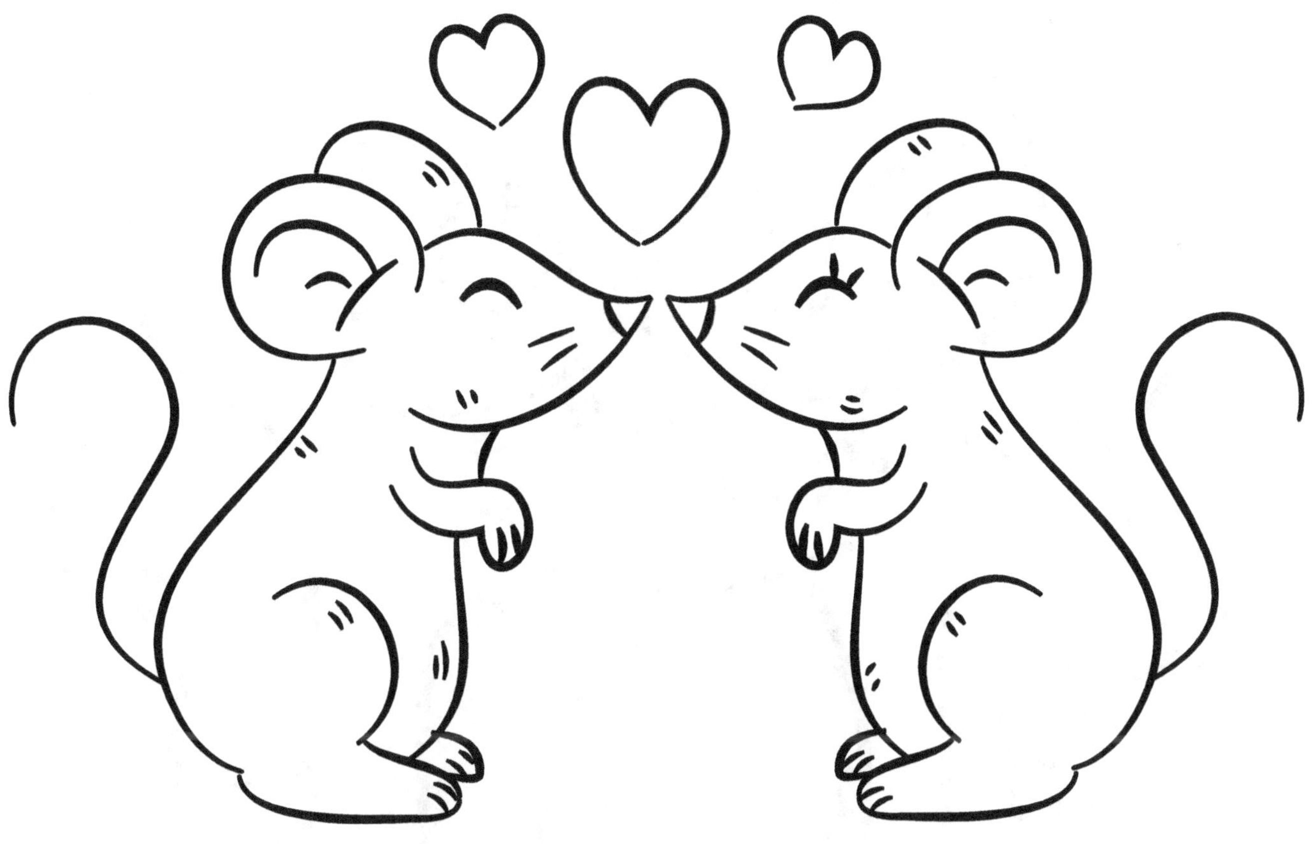

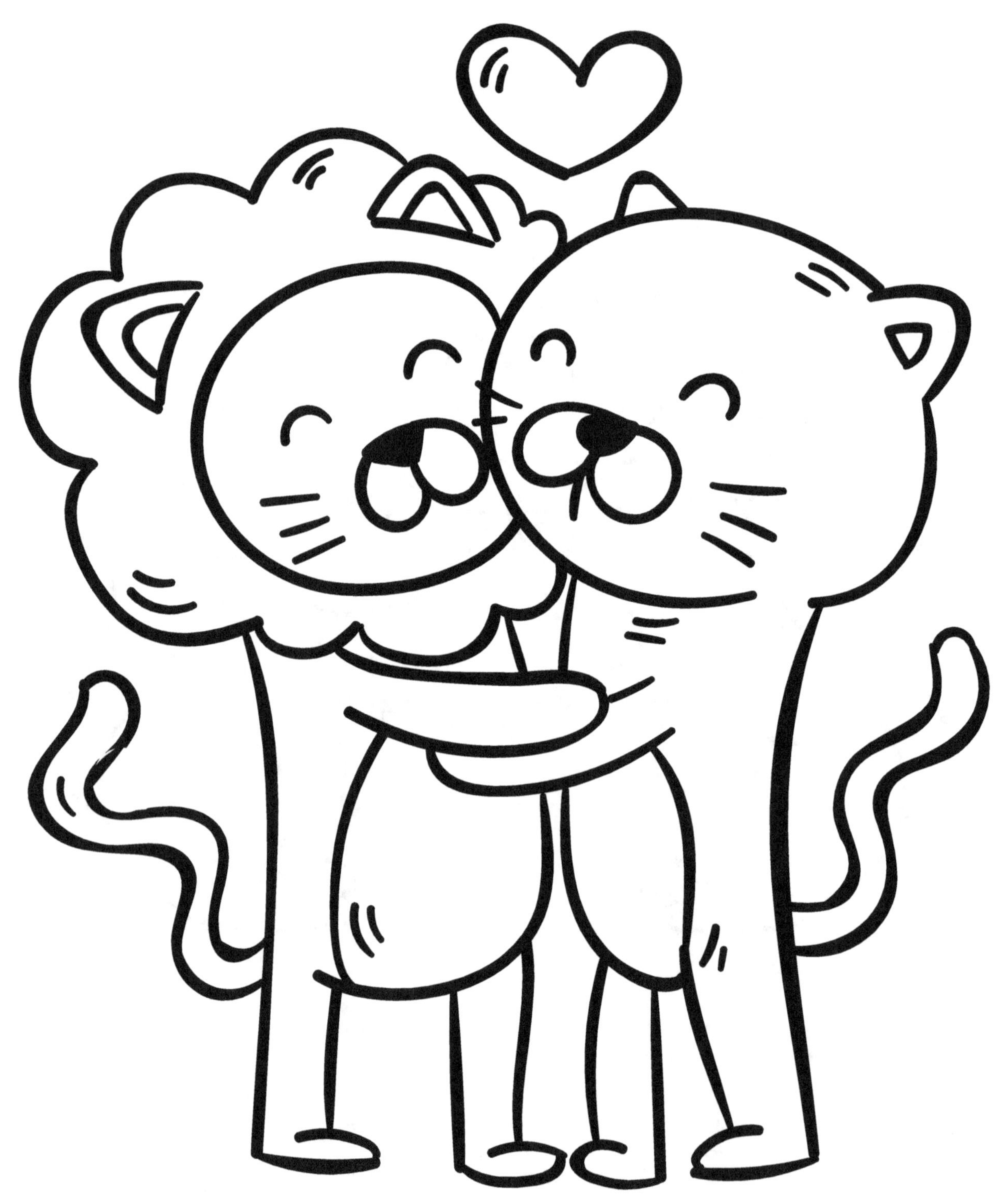

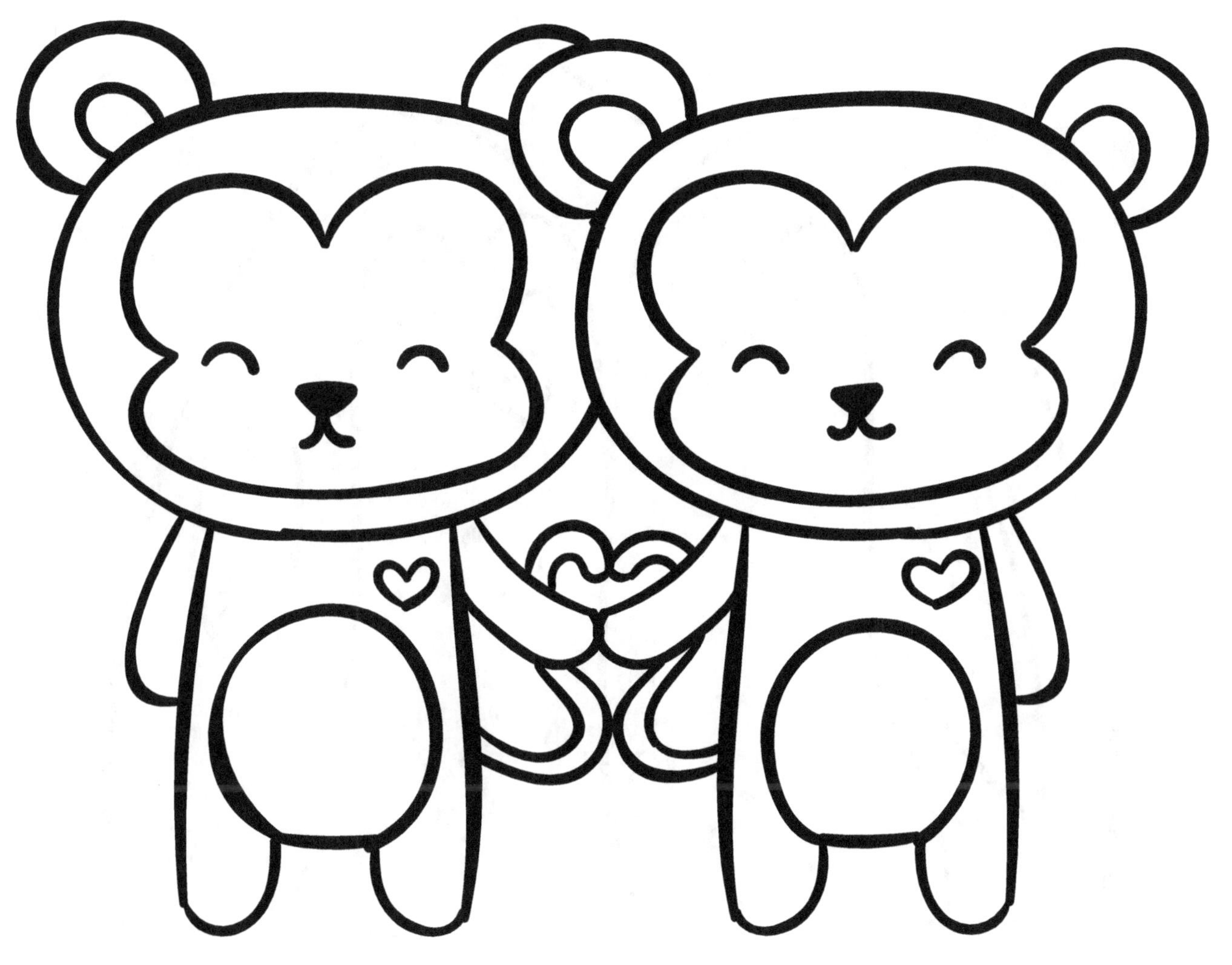

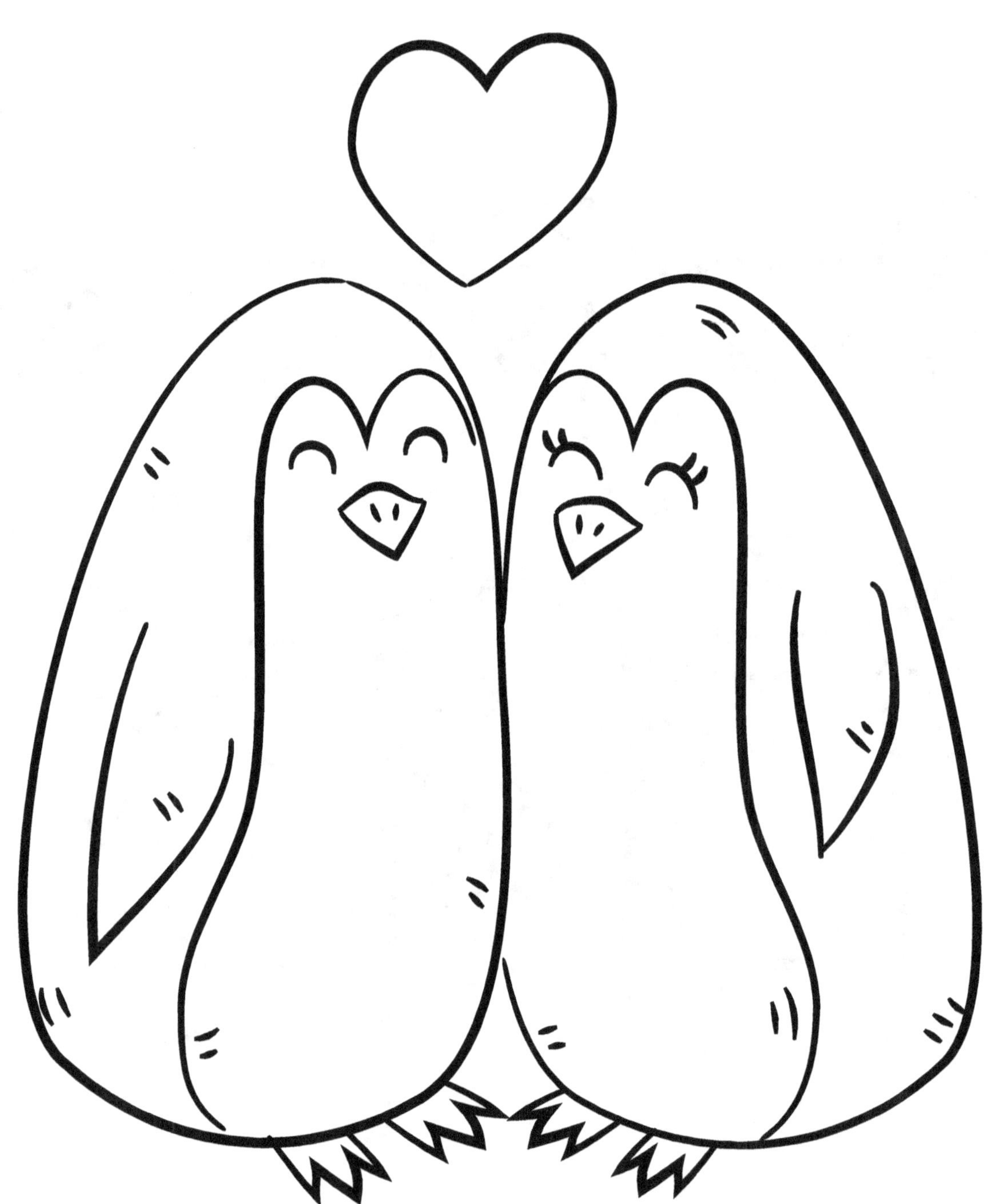

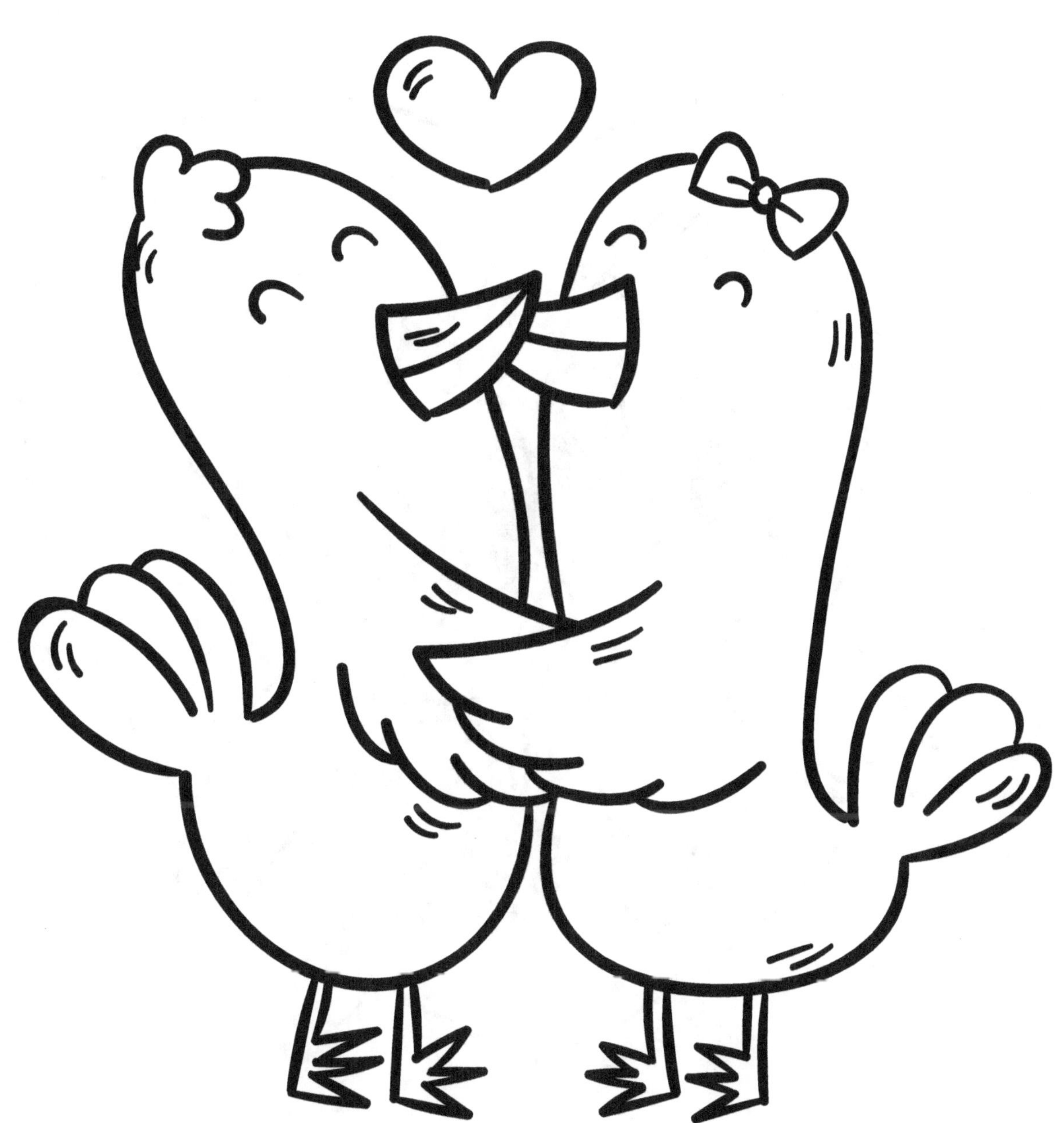

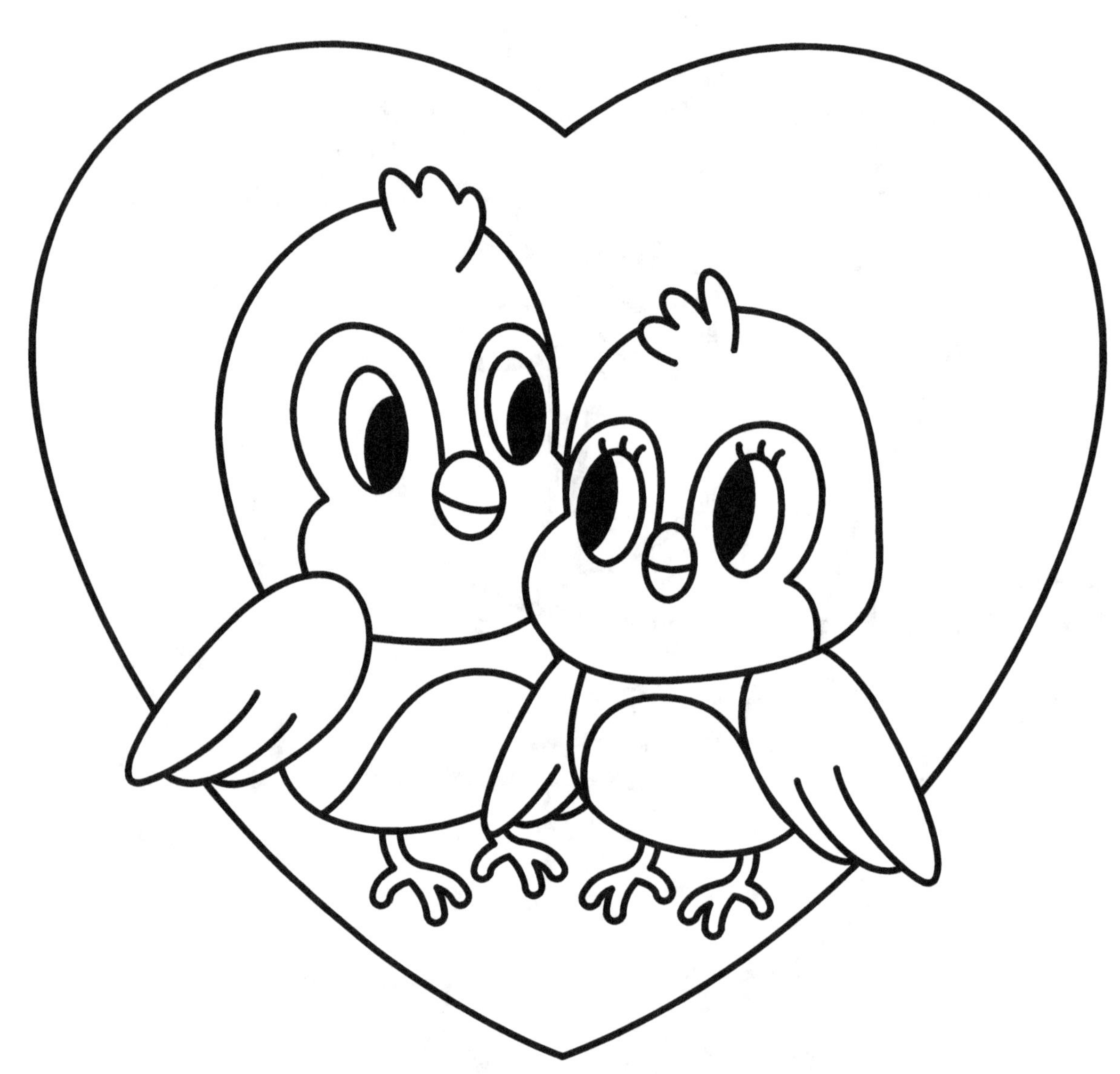

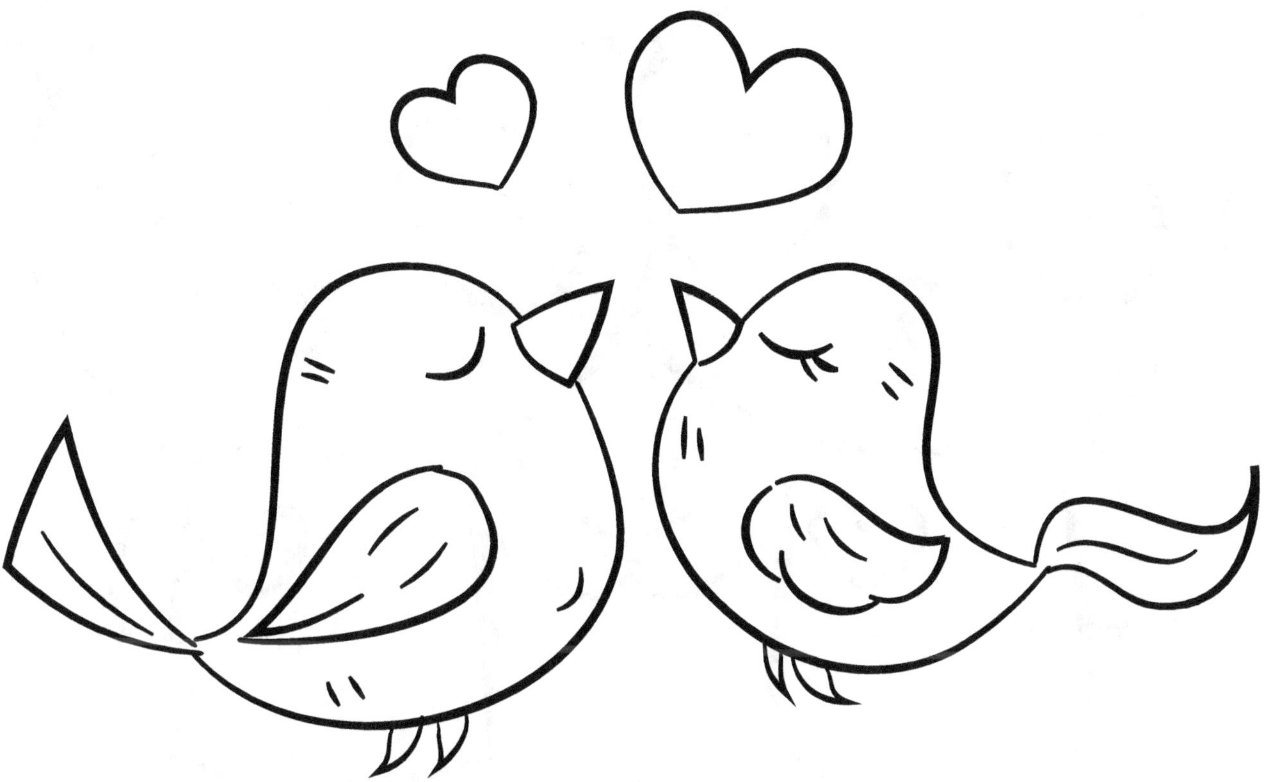

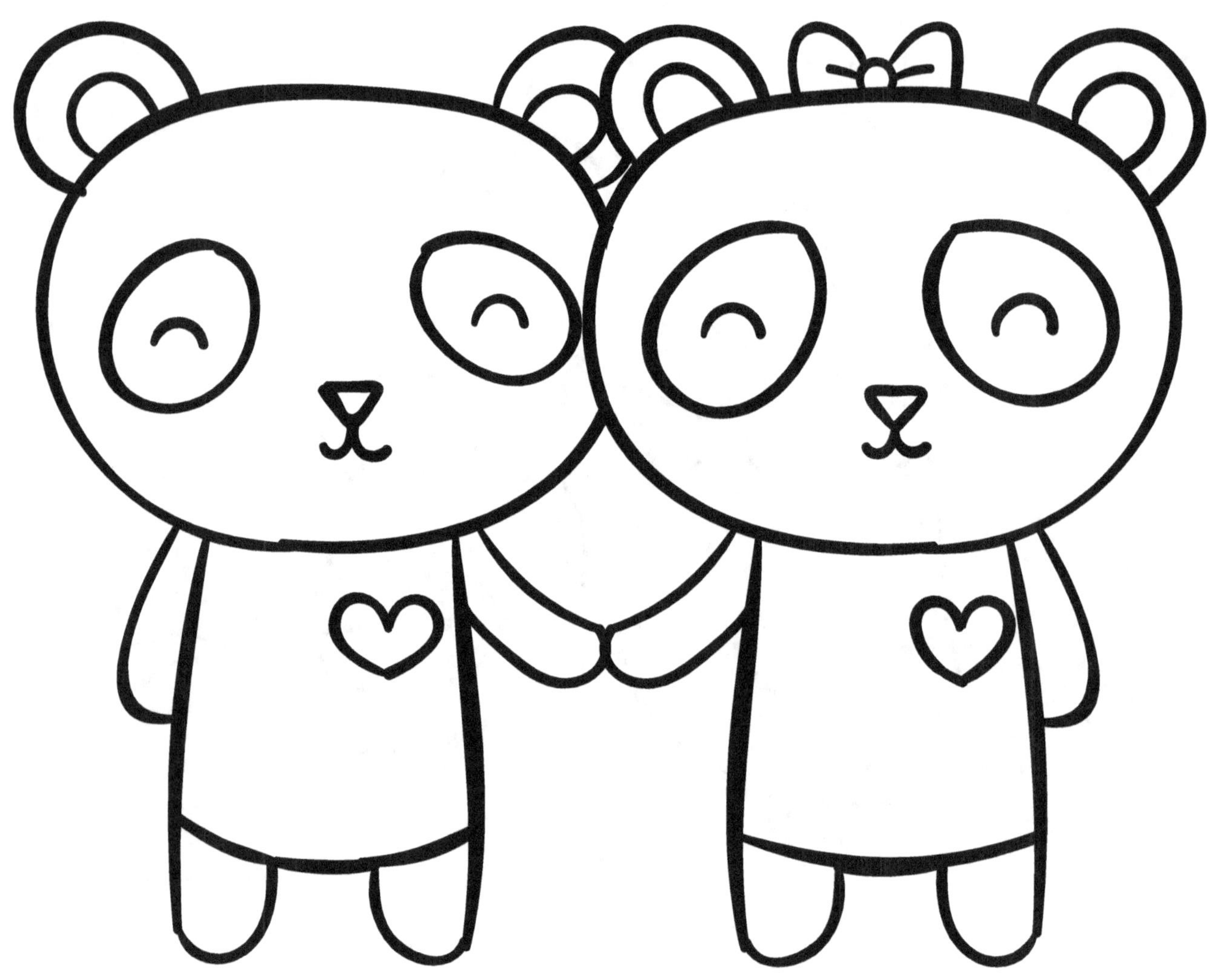

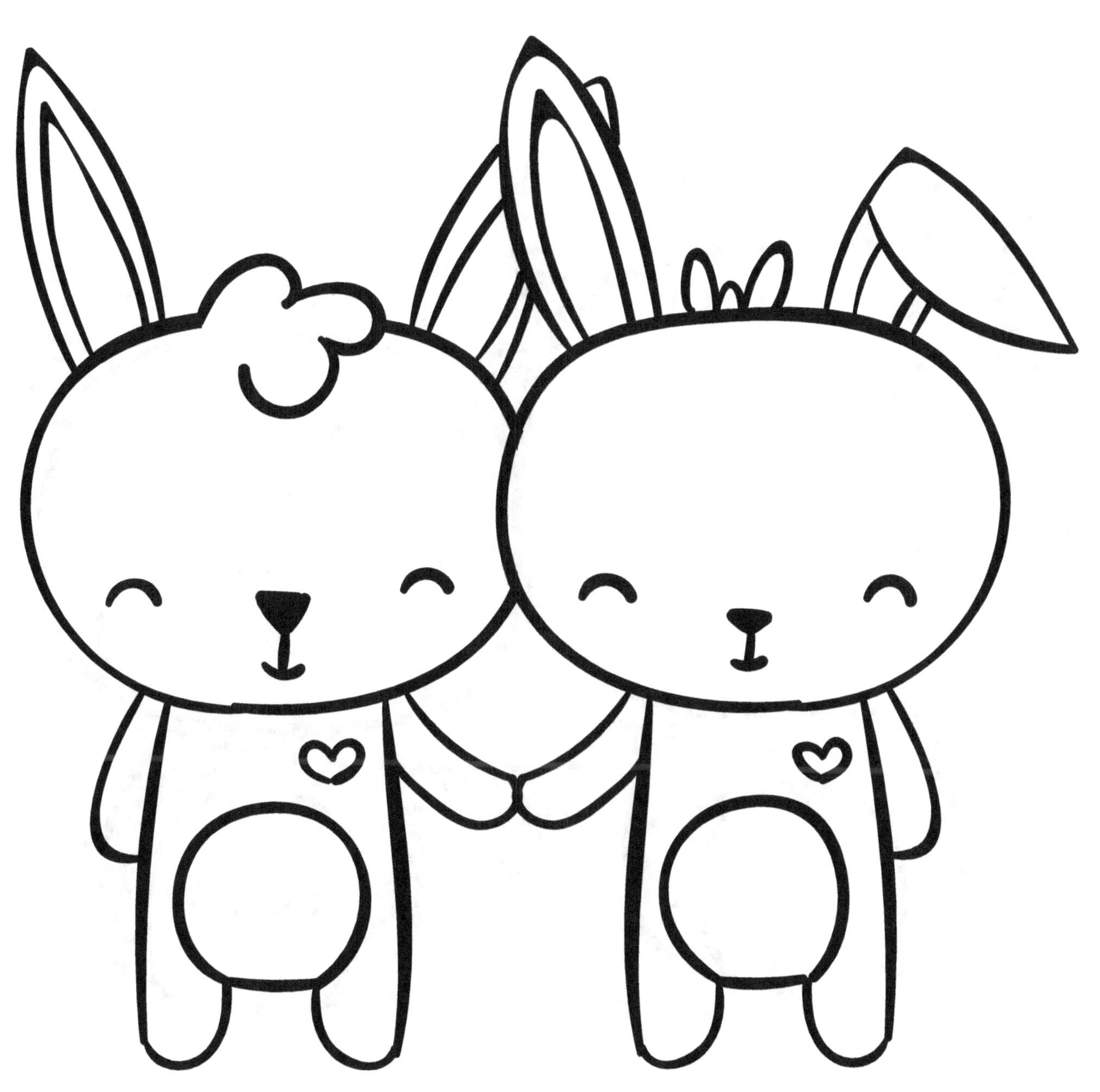

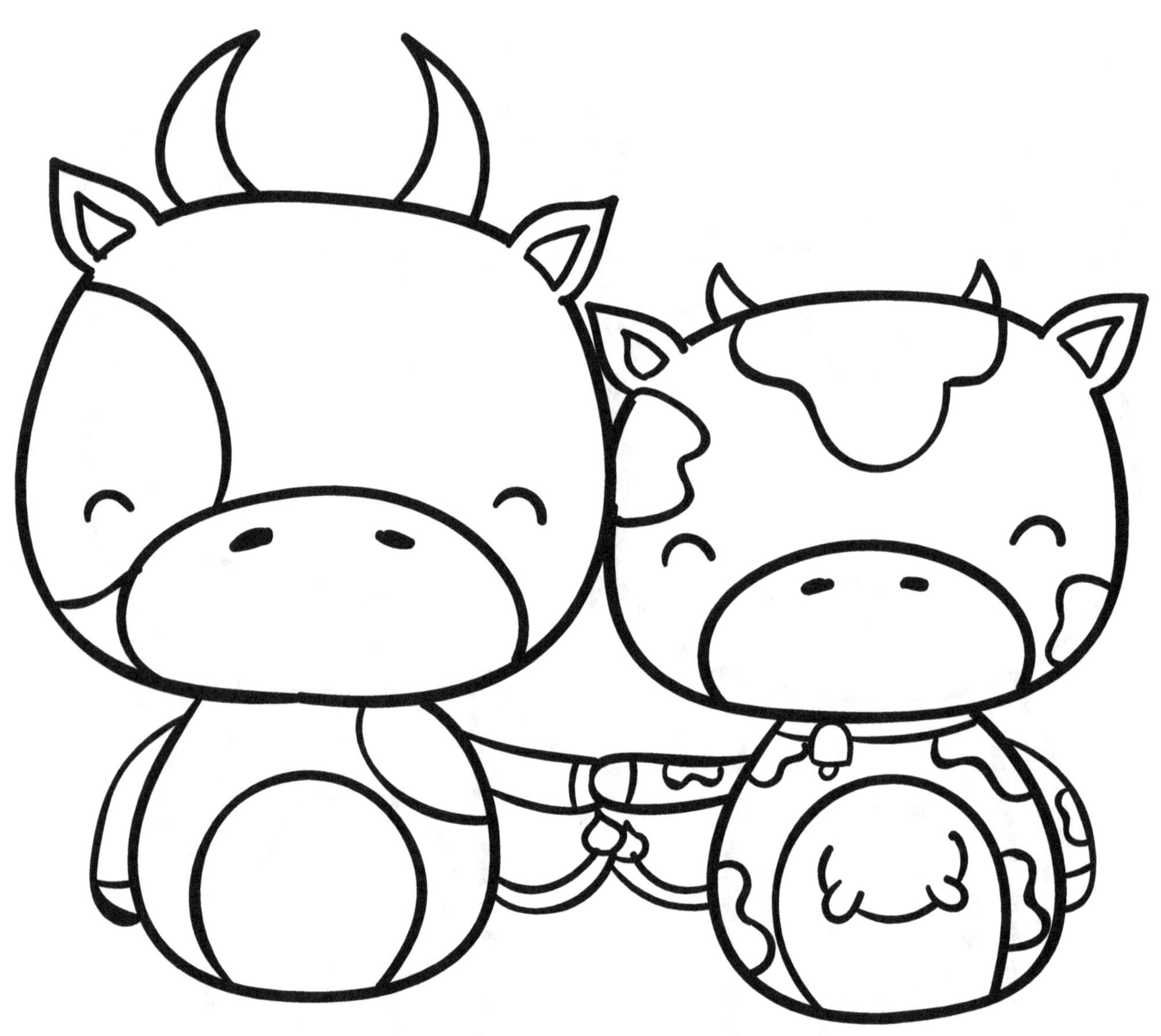

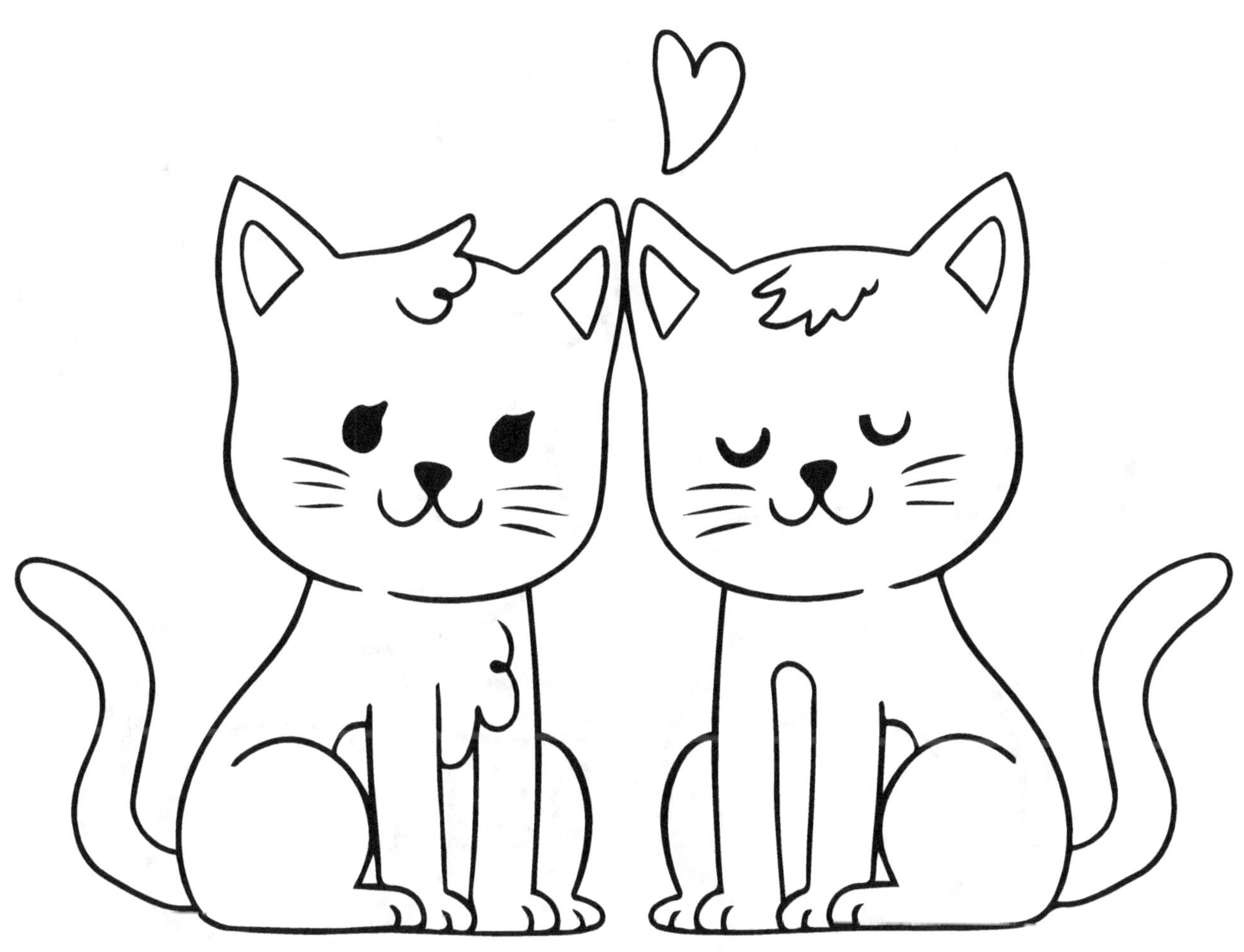

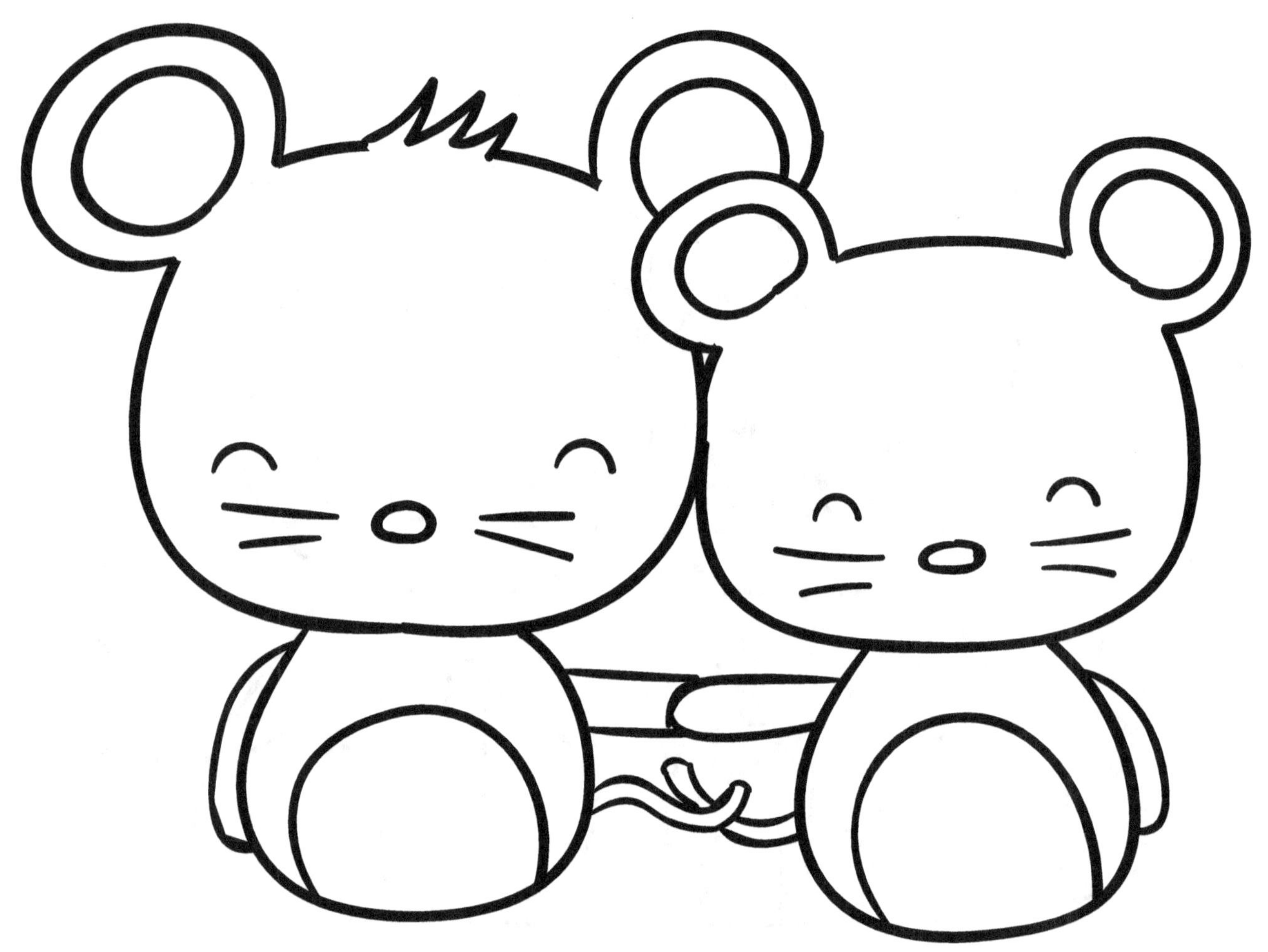

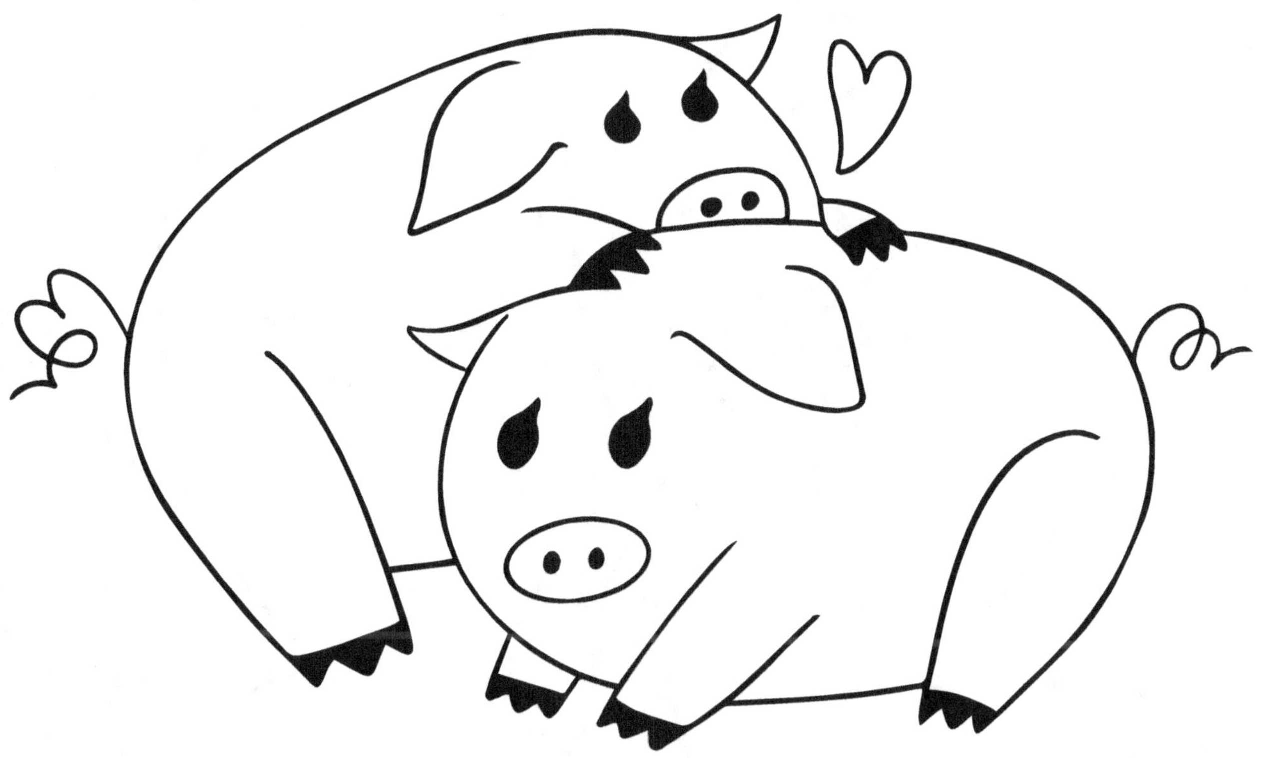

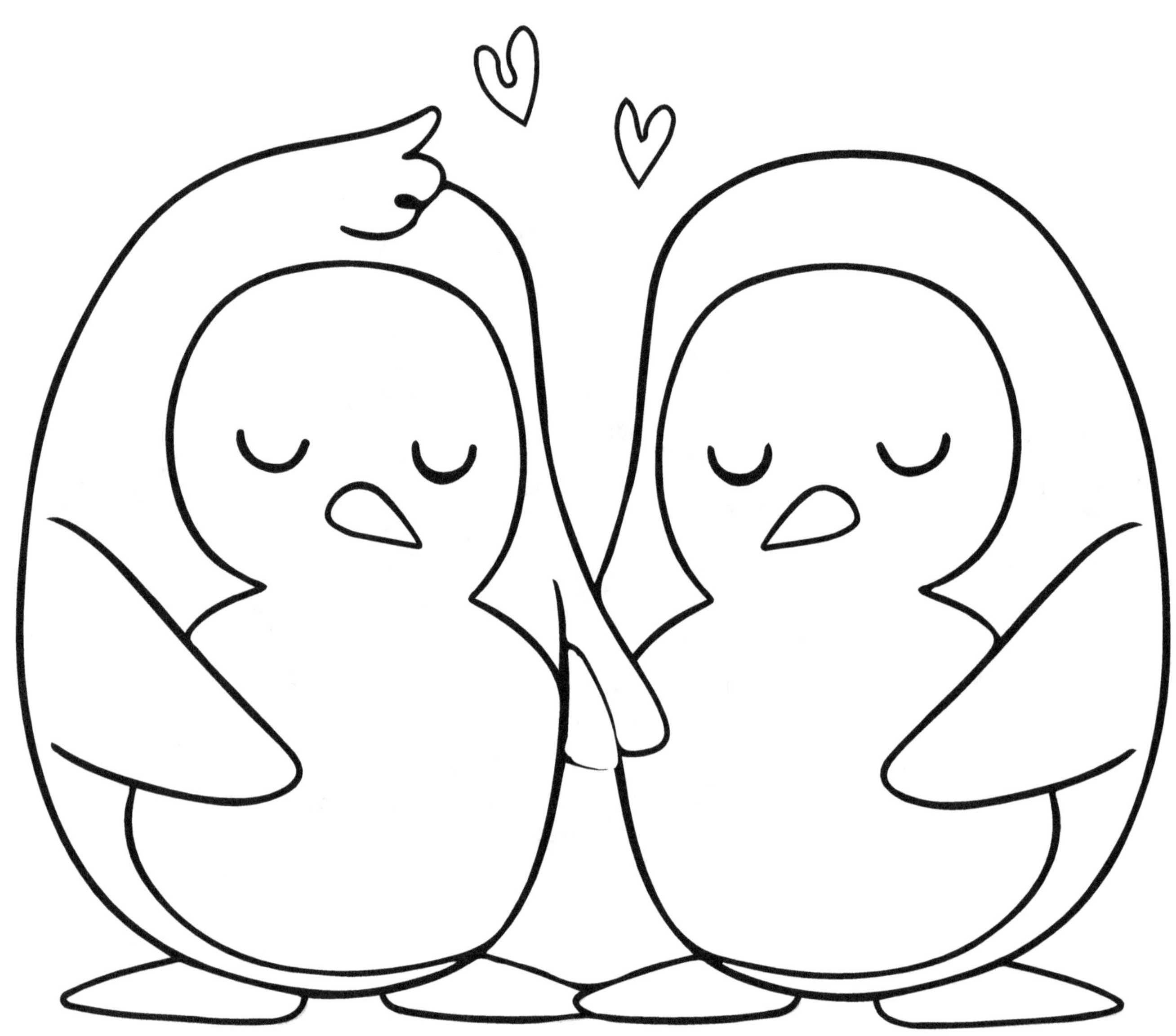

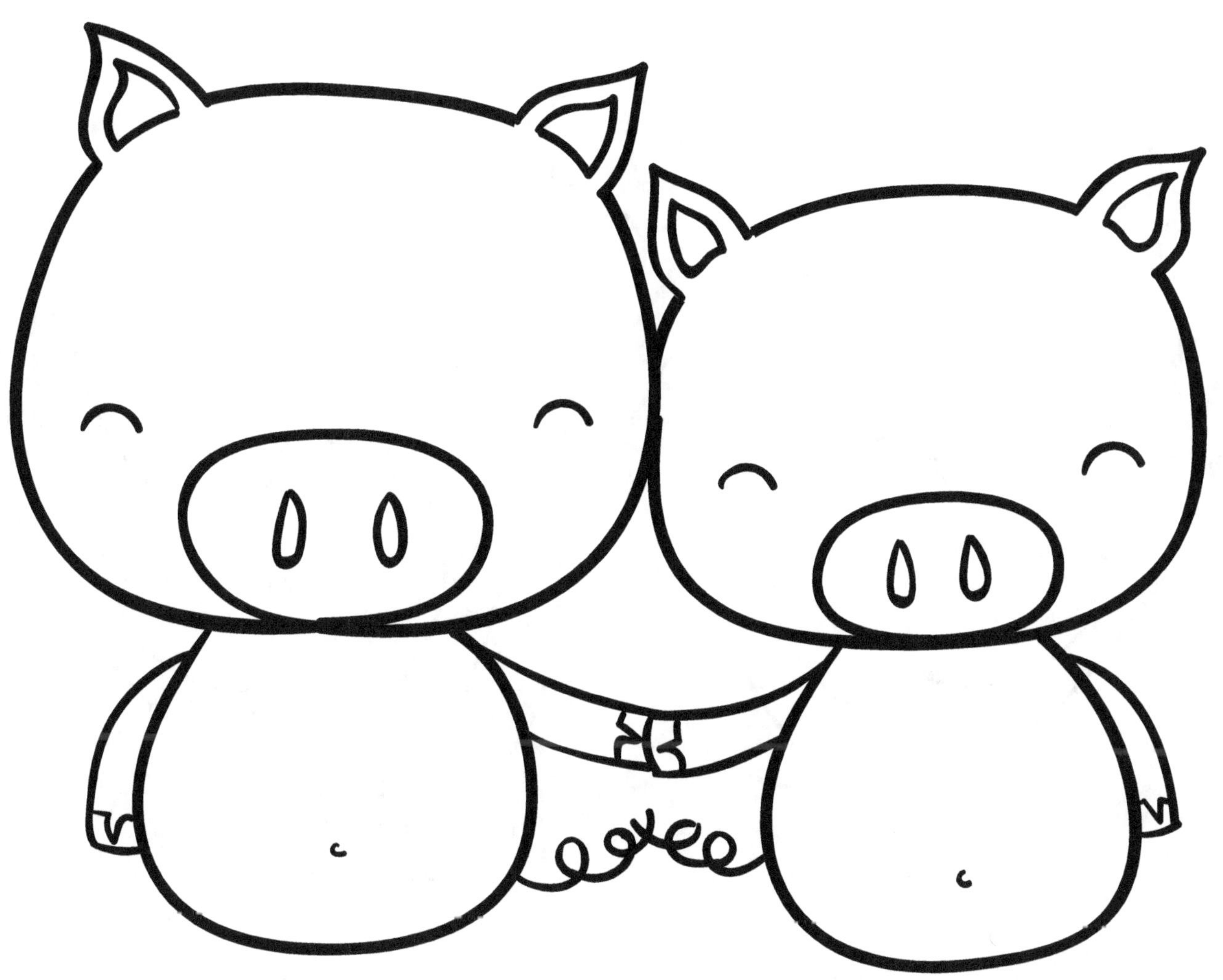

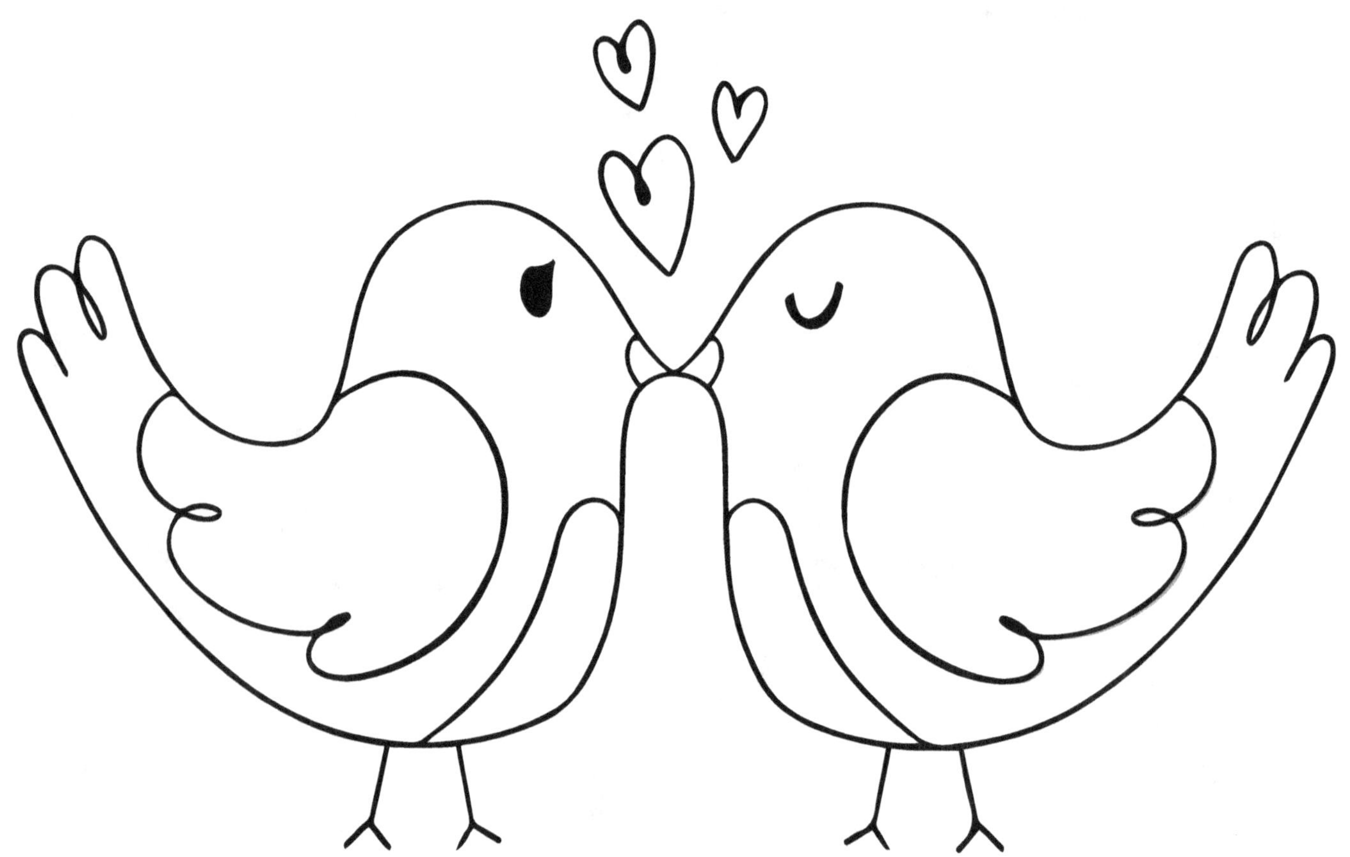

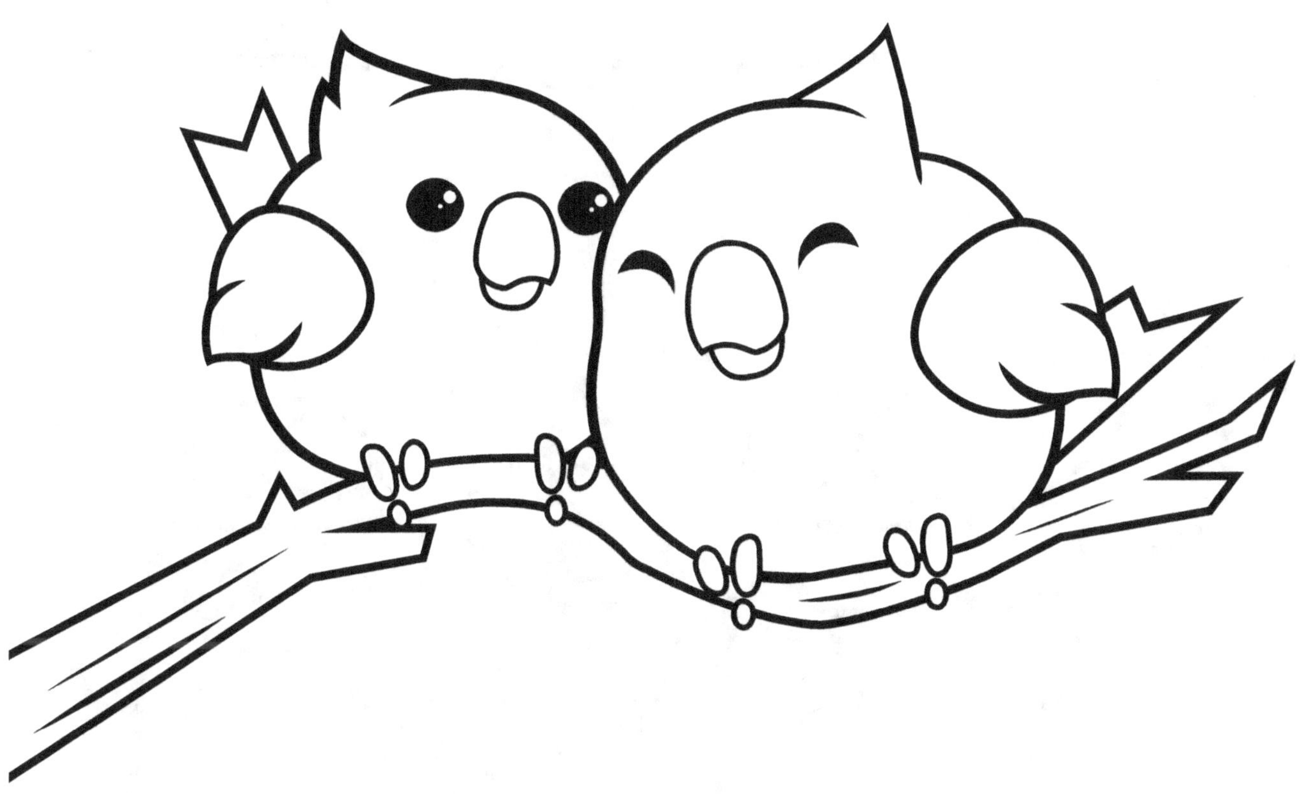

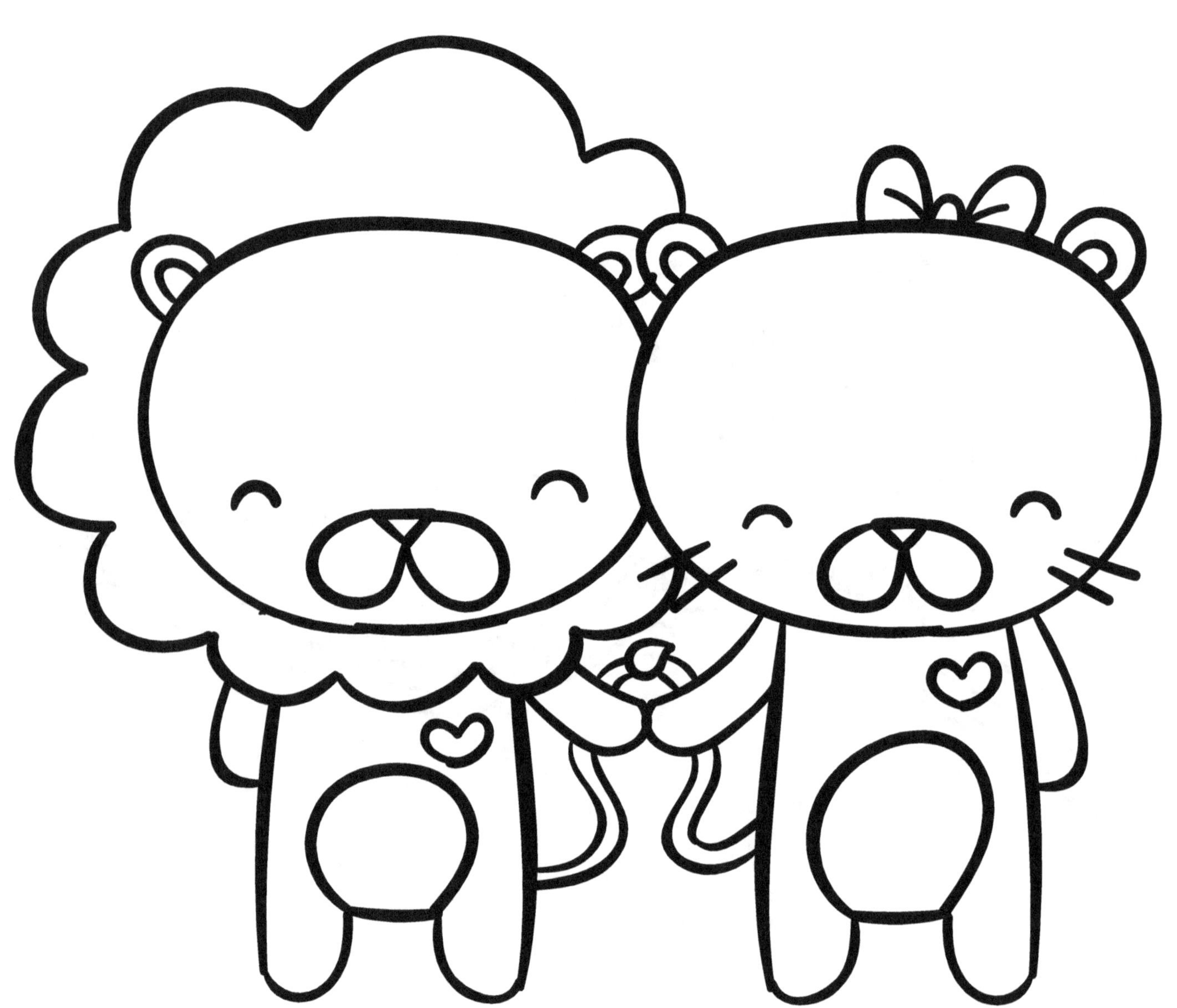

www.ingramcontent.com/pod-product-compliance
Lightning Source LLC
Chambersburg PA
CBHW081023260726
48662CB00026B/3019